THE GIFT OF THE TORTOISE

NEW INSIGHTS INTO THE I CHING

Jo Onvlee and Amy Shapiro, M. Ed.

THE GIFT OF THE TORTOISE: NEW INSIGHTS INTO THE I CHING

Copyright © 2011 Amy Shapiro, M. Ed.

All rights reserved.

Inquiries may be directed at www.NewAgeSages.com

ISBN-13: 978-1461090403
ISBN-10: 1461090407

THE GIFT OF THE TORTOISE: NEW INSIGHTS INTO THE I CHING

CONTENTS

	Introduction	1
Chapter 1	Quantifying Time	3
Chapter 2	Gathering Momentum	15
Chapter 3	Trioles	25
Chapter 4	Hearing the Oracle	37
Chapter 5	Patterns	49
Chapter 6	Divisions and the Star	73
Chapter 7	Reverse and Interim Hexagrams	87
Chapter 8	Triole Sums	105
Chapter 9	Tri-une Triplets and the Emperor	131
Chapter 10	Parallels and a Parable	149
	Appendix: Models for Further Study	157
	Glossary	161
	Index	165
	Bibliography	167
	Hexagram Cards	173
	About the Authors	177

INTRODUCTION

Chaos theory holds that **chaos,** once thought a 'chaotic' occurrence, viewed as out of place and without purpose – is in fact a predictable part of the natural order of things; not disrupting order, but part of a larger system beyond the ordinary scope. In China, as well as in the West, highly intelligent people interested in the **how** and **why** of our existence, have concluded that the Great Laws beyond everyday manifestations are not chaotic. Yet, for the average person, *chaos* is a real everyday phenomenon, and as did peasants of ancient China, we still today search for a coherent picture and possible solutions to our daily problems.

Sages laid down a way to deal with what was commonly viewed as 'chaotic' in an ancient philosophical treatise – the I CHING. Through the ages, and still today, practitioners of divination seek counsel and wisdom in the I Ching's Judgments. Beautifully stated, with omens and phrases from other classics, the I Ching has achieved a stature of high esteem, worldwide. For most practitioners, the I Ching is a means to arrive at a deeper appreciation of the greater flow of energies, whereby we may commune with our essentially spiritual natures.

As many translations of the Chinese masterpieces are available, there is no need for a new translation. THE GIFT OF THE TORTOISE is not a new translation but offers new ways of seeing into the **core** of the I Ching, the Hexagrams themselves, the lines, the construction of an oracle, and what it can say to us in the modern world.

Readers who have absorbed the concepts and theories in our basic text, QUESTIONING THE ORACLE: THE I CHING, are prepared to delve into new riddles in these pages, such as: is there a secret behind the Textual number? Is there a reason behind the changes?

These and many other questions kept us on a search for answers. As co-authors, we combined insights gained over decades of metaphysical study. Of course, we don't have all the answers! But, as the I CHING says, when in balance with the natural order of things, it furthers one to "cross the great waters". These words have a profound depth and challenge us to liberate ourselves from the confines of narrow viewpoints, to reach the ultimate goal; union with the flow of Chi and communion with one's formless Spirit. So, we thought we'd let you know, with great pleasure and honor, what we have received from

THE GIFT OF THE TORTOISE.

CHAPTER 1: QUANTIFYING TIME

A popular Chinese legend tells of a Sage named Fu His who, while contemplating the patterns of cracks on the carapace covering the back of a tortoise, discovered the meaning of the endless changes of the I Ching. While the tortoise shell is symbolically significant, it is possible to delve into more abstract reasoning within the concepts expressed through the I Ching. Our purpose here is to explore the inner workings of that remarkable Chinese legacy, with a unique approach.

Let us first imagine that the following succession of short lines (Fig. 1.1) represents a series of **Moments** upon a kind of **Timeline** of our experiences, extending from past (left) to future (right).

- -

Figure 1.1

Think now of Time as making little **jumps** between moments. Each moment's **quantum** may be imperceptibly small or perceived as a big lump. Each jump occurs between perceivable quanta; thus, its content is unknown to us. Let us call what happens therein **un-time. Un-time** is unknown and incomprehensible. Just as **no time** opposes and compliments our experience of time, it is also akin to what we mean when we refer to something as occurring in an **untimely** manner. Even when one is **on time**, the awareness of the passage of time is often almost non-existent.

Time, therefore, in addition to matter and energetic processes, is quantifiable. A Time-quantum is the smallest amount of time that one can perceive and measure, with a value that can be experienced as active or passive, strong or weak. The Chinese call these values **Yang** or **Yin**. They use as symbols for these an unbroken and a broken line, (Fig. 1.2).

Yang = ▬▬▬   Yin = ▬ ▬

Figure 1.2

Therewith, we arrive at the I Ching, which purports to tell us that the endless *changing* moments of Yang and Yin are meaningful and form characteristic patterns, related to universally observable changes. A pattern or set of time-quantum can thereby be considered to be *creative* or *receptive*, winning or losing, etc.

Let us go deeper into these *characteristic* patterns of time-quanta and how they came to be recognized. Certain happenings change our *histories*, and if they hadn't happened, our lives would be different, our *present* being a result of our history. Each of our *stories* seem to be ruled, and even prognosticated by, those various Yang or Yin time-value differences.

If we now **blow up** our Time-line, our Moments become containers, shown below as a series of boxes (Fig. 1.3). Each is open to **contain** a Yang force or a Yin force, the determination of which is the subject of many disciplines, intended to enable one to predict the correlating happening.

Figure 1.3

An endless row of moments, of course, both precede and follow any representative portion of our time line compartments, in which we now randomly place the Yang and Yin symbols (Fig. 1.4), one to a box. Thus, if we focus on only one moment-box, we observe its contents to be either Yang or Yin. In actuality, the Chinese have identified many lists of things that they consider to be Yang or Yin.

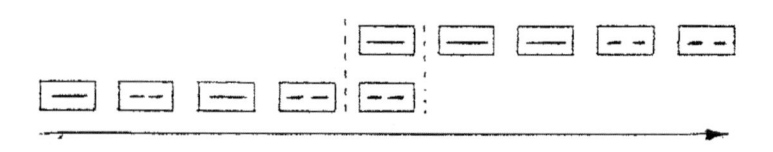

Figure 1.4

Let us go one step further, to add a nuance to this simple vision, and consider two boxes simultaneously, starting with a Yang or Yin box and **compressing** two boxes within a time-quantum (Fig. 1.5), by **stepping** up or down.

Stepping up:

Stepping down:

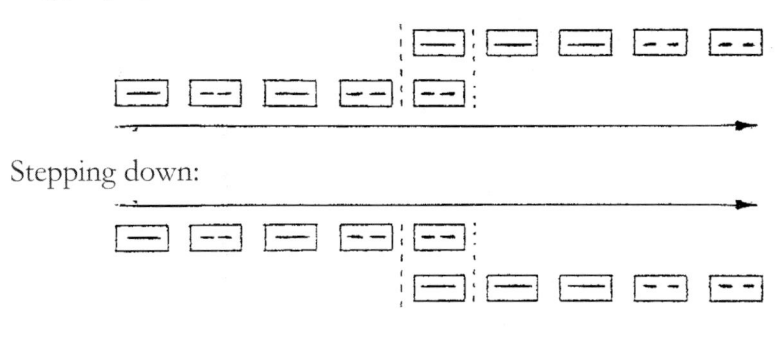

Figure 1.5

If we begin stepping down from the opposite value, Yang instead of Yin, the resulting sets of moment-boxes (Fig. 1.6) look alike:

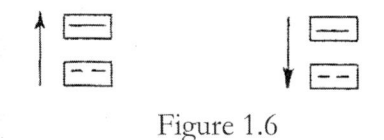

Figure 1.6

Here is our Time line, from a strictly directional perspective (Fig. 1.7):

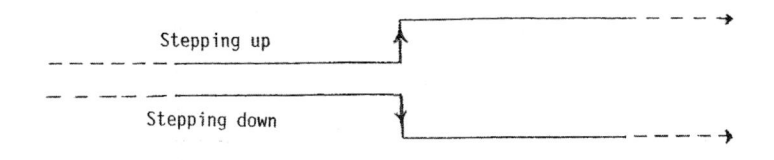

Figure 1.7

By combining Yang _____ and Yin __ __ Monograms through this stepping process, four different compressed Time-quanta, or quanta

Bigrams (Fig. 1.8) evolve. The Chinese call these abstract Bigrams the **elements**:

Figure 1.8

Further, if we digitalize Yin and Yang, with Yin being Zero (akin to potentials) and Yang being One (akin to actualization), we can state:

From 0 to 1 = stepping up

And from 1 to 0 = stepping down

This, in itself, falls yet again in a Yang or Yin category, as we notice how, with stepping up, time-quanta build up from below, and with stepping down, time-quanta are built from above (Fig. 1.9).

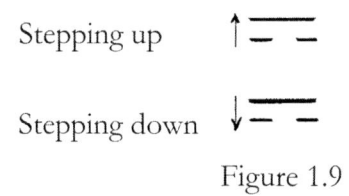

Stepping up

Stepping down

Figure 1.9

While these two different **moments** look alike on the surface, with the same monograms in the same visual order, the relativity of their being stepped-up or stepped-down creates a difference in their symbolic impacts. As it is possible to meet a Yang or a Yin in either position, so too, a **positive** and a **negative** logic exists (Fig. 1.10). We say, for instance: "That cup is half full" or "It is half empty."

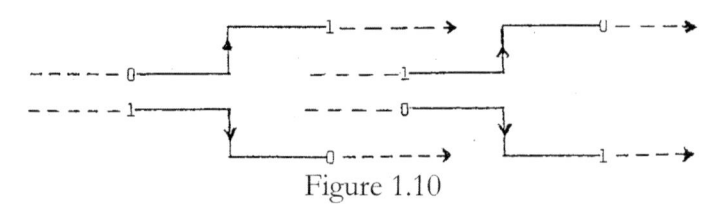

Figure 1.10

The evolution of the two time-moment monograms into four time-moment bigrams gives rise to elemental philosophical reasoning, such as the four basic directions or four basic elements (Fig 1.11), as understood by ancient people.

☰
☷   ☳

☷

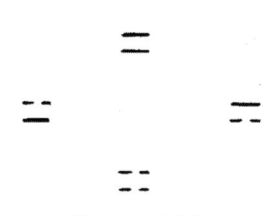

Figure 1.11

But **Life** is far more differentiated in its manifold aspects, requiring us to go a step further to obtain more nuances. Let us now compress one more box within the same time quantum (Fig. 1.12), once again by stepping up and stepping down.

Stepping up

Stepping down

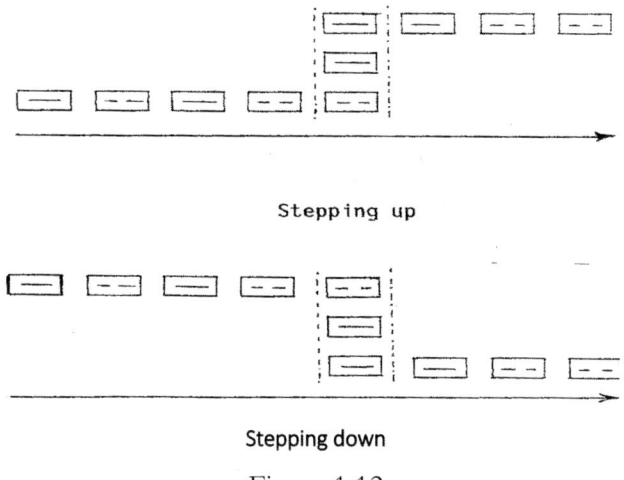

Figure 1.12

By thus compressing a third Yang or Yin monogram within our four bigrams, we encounter eight possible Time-quanta or **trigrams** (Fig. 1.13). Stepping up or down, as we know, makes no visual difference.

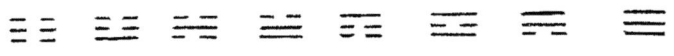

☷ ☶ ☵ ☳ ☴ ☲ ☱ ☰

Figure 1.13

The Chinese call these trigrams **the Eight directions** and place them around the compass, as shown in Figure 1.14.

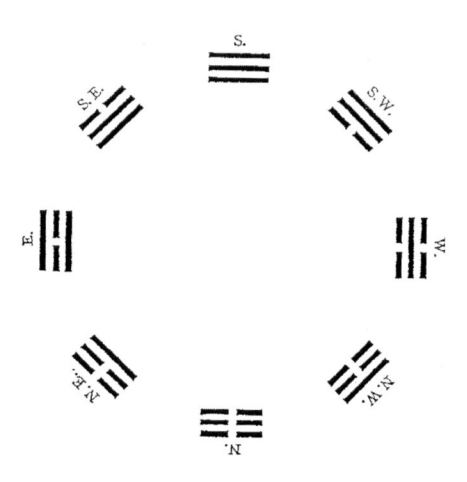

Figure 1.14

While the Chinese ascribe many meanings to these trigrams, we have not yet satisfied our need for more information. The great many lists of the Chinese show us that to interpret life with it is a complicated matter, requiring still more hooks upon which to hang life's many nuances and subtleties.

We can simplify our previous time-line, expressing the possible filling of time-moments with Yang and Yin, using a time Horizon, (Fig. 1.15).

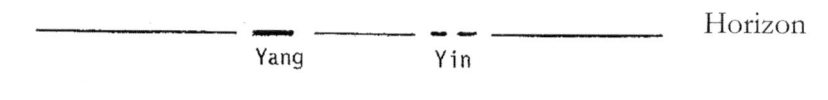

Figure 1.15

To that, we shall add a **curve-line** above the time-line (Fig. 1.16), using a series of dashes:

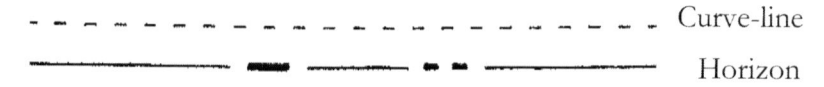

Figure 1.16

Our first time-component compression causes our curve-line to arc (Fig. 1.17).

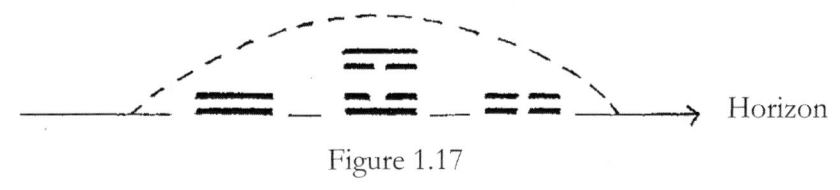

Figure 1.17

This simple example of the probability theory shows that the middle combinations have twice as much chance of turning up as do either of the end combinations. Expressed as a formula:

$$\text{Monogram} + 1 = \text{Bigram}.$$

The number of ways that bigrams can occur is: 1, 2, 1 because:

$$(1+1)^2 = (1+1)(1+1) = 1 + 2 + 1$$

Just as modern electronics uses only digital information (1 and 0), we can write and express everything as ⎯⎯ and ⎯ ⎯, or by substitution we can present ⎯⎯ = a, and ⎯ ⎯ = b.

From: $(a + b)^2 = (a + b)(a + b)$
$$= a^2 + ba + ab + b^2$$

We derive (Fig. 1.18):

Figure 1.18

Carrying on with the same formula: Bigram + 1 = Trigram

The number of ways trigrams can occur is: 1, 3, 3, 1

Because: $(1+1)^3 = (1+1)(1+1)(1+1) = 1 + 3 + 3 + 1.$
If, again: ⎯⎯ = a and ⎯ ⎯ = b,
Then $(a + b)^3 = (a + b)^2 (a + b)$
$$= (a^2 + ba + ab + b^2)(a + b)$$
$$= aaa + baa + aba + bba + aab + bab + abb + bbb$$

Thus, also (Fig. 1.19)…

$$(— + -- --)^3 = (— + -- --)^2(— + -- --)$$

Figure 1.19

Trigrams with **either** one Yang or one Yin line have a 6-to-1 chance of occurring, while the odds of a trigram having only two Yang and one Yin, or only two Yin and one Yang, are 3-to-1 (Fig. 1.20).

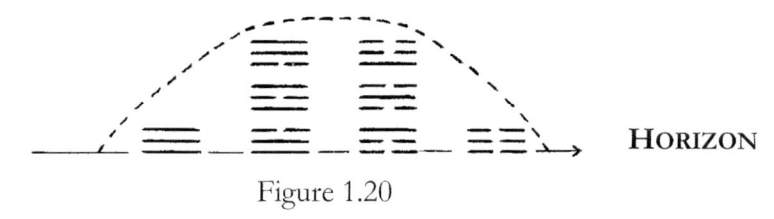

Figure 1.20

The more time moments fold together in one view, the closer our curve resembles the normal bell curve found in probability theory. If we now fold together four time-quanta, the resulting form is:

Trigram + 1 = Tetragram.

The number of ways Tetragrams can occur is: 1 + 4 + 6 + 4 + 1 = 16.

Further, the folding of time moments follows this progression:

For	Monograms	$2 = 2^1$
	Bigrams	$4 = 2^2$
	Trigrams	$8 = 2^3$
	Tetragrams	$16 = 2^4$
	Pentagrams	$32 = 2^5$
	Hexagrams	$64 = 2^6$

As we are studying the I Ching, our interest in this progression goes only as far as Hexagrams, which the Chinese people have long used to achieve a high quality of prognostication. Other people of antiquity devised forms of prognoses in this progression; Africans used a set of 16 Tetragrams called **Ifa**, and Europeans used a set of 32 Pentagrams since the Middle Ages, although their predictive system was arguably trivial.

The curve of possible Hexagrams (Fig. 1.21) almost matches the normal curve with the form, 1 + 6 + 15 + 20 + 15 + 6 + 1 = 64

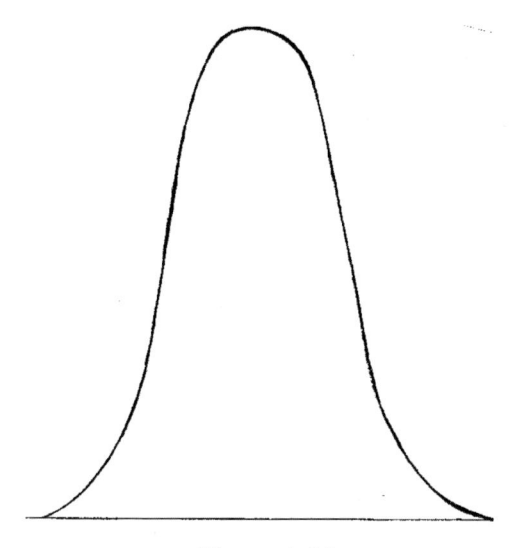

Figure 1.21

The amount of Yang lines in various sets can be stated:

Monograms	1 with	1 Yang line
	1 with	0 Yang lines (1 Yin line)
Bigrams	1 with	2 Yang lines
	2 with	1 Yang line
	1 with	0 Yang lines
Trigrams	1 with	3 Yang lines
	3 with	2 Yang lines
	3 with	1 Yang line
	1 with	0 Yang lines
Tetragrams	1 with	4 Yang lines
	4 with	3 Yang lines
	6 with	2 Yang lines
	4 with	1 Yang line
	1 with	0 Yang lines

Pentagrams	1 with	5 Yang lines
	5 with	4 Yang lines
	10 with	3 Yang lines
	10 with	2 Yang lines
	5 with	1 Yang line
	1 with	0 Yang lines
Hexagrams	1 with	6 Yang lines
	6 with	5 Yang lines
	15 with	4 Yang lines
	20 with	3 Yang lines
	15 with	2 Yang lines
	6 with	1 Yang line
	1 with	0 Yang lines

This mathematical progression continues, and perhaps other systems of prognostication exist that use greater sets. The progression follows the binomial expansion known as **Pascal's Triangle,** which displays the number of ways of choosing items from a set (Fig. 1.22).

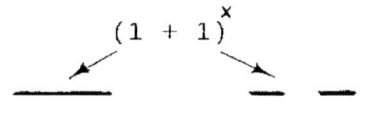

$$(1 + 1)^x$$

Figure 1.22:

Shown in progression (Fig. 1.23), it looks like this:

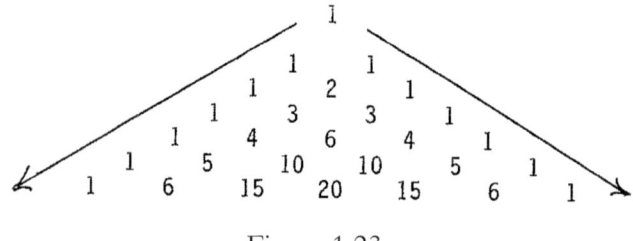

```
                    1
                  1   1
                1   2   1
              1   3   3   1
            1   4   6   4   1
          1   5  10  10   5   1
        1   6  15  20  15   6   1
```

Figure 1.23

And the series continues. If we want to know, for example, how many time-quanta in a certain set have a certain number of Yang lines, we can use the following permutation formula.

Let X = the number of quanta taken together in one view
and Y = the number of Yang lines specified;
(**C** is the variable we seek and '!' symbolizes **factorial**)

Then:

$$_{X}^{Y}C = \frac{X!}{Y!\,(Y-X)!}$$

If we have a set of Hexagrams, then X = 6, and if we want to know how many sets contain 3 Yang lines, then Y = 3, thus:

$$_{6}^{3}C = \frac{6!}{3!\,(6-3)!} = \frac{6 \times 5 \times 4 \times 3 \times 2 \times 1}{(3 \times 2 \times 1)(3 \times 2 \times 1)} = 20$$

Thus, 20 Hexagrams (Fig. 1.24) each contain 3 Yang lines.

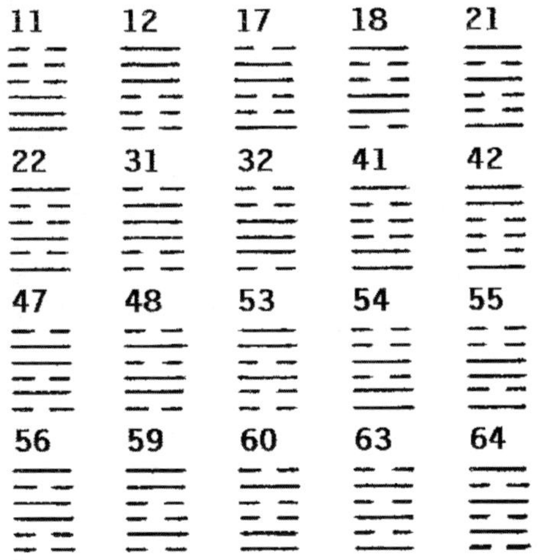

Figure 1.24

CHAPTER 2: GATHERING MOMENTUM

To review what we have thus far accomplished, we return to the first Time line image (Fig. 2.1), which is still the most intriguing concept.

Figure 2.1

Widening our viewpoint by **blowing up** the Time line a little, we understood each moment as having the potential for active and passive impulses. Then, by a kind of stepping process, we saw how multiple time quanta values can exist simultaneously. Yet, as time continues unperceived between quanta, looking at one vertical figure representing a Time quanta series (Fig. 2.2) does not tell us if it occurred by stepping up or stepping down.

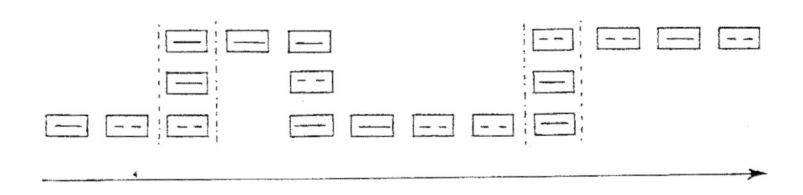

Figure 2.2

If we focus upon only those vertical figures, so the rest goes completely out of view, the following series of **compressed** time quanta values (Fig. 2.3) remain in view:

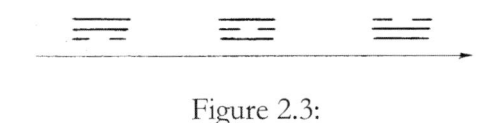

Figure 2.3:

More accurately, our stepping process resembles a spiraling movement (Fig. 2.4), as time coils through our figures, descending in the front and rising up in the back:

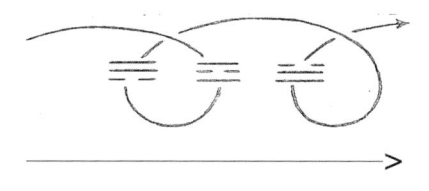

Figure 2.4:

When a full set becomes known, its beginning and end may be joined, whether or not it happens naturally. The well-known circle of Fu His, (Fig. 2.5) places the sixty-four Hexagram patterns in a circle, sequenced so as to correctly show time flowing forth in a mathematical, **binary**, progression. Positioning the mirror-opposite Hexagrams to face one another at opposite points across the circle, this mysterious Sage achieved an ideal balance and symmetry.

Hexagram 1 = 111111 in Binary, which is the Numerical Sum 63.
Hexagram 2 = 000000 in Binary, which is the Numerical Sum 0.
Hexagram 2 and 1 thus naturally oppose each other on the wheel.

Figure 2.5:

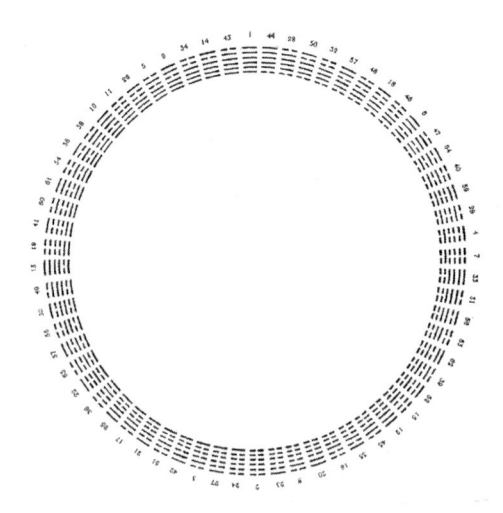

Yet, the beauty of Fu Hsi's symmetrical arrangement of Hexagrams does not hide the fact that the numbers assigned to the Hexagrams do not reflect their mathematical equivalents. Tradition holds that the numbers were given in such an order by the legendary King Wen, Duke of Chou.

"But, why?" I (Jo) wondered. And, herein hangs a tale of an odyssey that is both personal and metaphysical, as this strange feature of the I Ching set me on an unusual search to find the answer.

So, I approached the I Ching with an inquiring mind, not prone to using it as an advisor. And through this different way of looking, I came to a number of conclusions, which I have not found discussed, nor even mentioned, in any other source. Like anyone, I learned to form a Hexagram by the simple method of coin tossing or a more elaborate method with yarrow stalks. When a Hexagram was formed, there regularly appeared one or more **changing** lines (Fig. 2.6), marked with either an x or an o, as for example:

Figure 2.6

What most struck me as curious was the fact that lines changed only in the initial Hexagram, but never in the second Hexagram, obtained from the first. Being mathematically minded, I reasoned:

If a Yin line is considered as 0 or 2, 8 or 6, it is even.
If a Yang line is considered as 1 or 3, 7 or 9, it is odd.

This led me back to digital reasoning and another approach. I wondered if, since, with **changing** lines, we must reckon with 4 quantities, if the number structure should also be 4-fold? No, I thought. Not so. Another train of thought proved very fruitful. We can see a number progression as an endless flow of alternating impulses of Yang and Yin. Let's say odd and even, as our decimal (base 10) figures 1 2 3 4 5 6 7 8 9 0 are considered alternately odd and even. In the binary (base 2) system, sequential numbers are expressed by writing 0, 1, 10, 11, 100, 101, etc.

Vertically, the Binary numbers are:		and equivalent to:
0	=	00
1	=	01
10	=	10
11	=	11

Separating the above right-hand column into two parts (Fig. 2.7), we glean a reason for the extra mark:

```
0 | 0 = even | even
0 | 1 = even | odd
1 | 0 = odd  | even
1 | 1 = odd  | odd
```

Figure 2.7

The first column is the unseen figure, while the second column is shown as value. This can also be written as Yang and Yin (Fig. 2.8).

```
00 = even | even = — — | — — = 0
01 = even | odd  = — — | ———  = 1
10 = odd  | even = ——— | — — = 2
11 = odd  | odd  = ——— | ———  = 3
```

Figure 2.8

Focusing on the right column of lines, it becomes clear that in order to visually differentiate the two Yin symbols (— — with a value of 2, and — — with a value of 0), the value-2 Yin line must carry a mark to signify the Yang line in the column to its left. The same applies to the two Yang lines of differing values.

So, out of necessity, the lines for binary 10 and 11 carry their unseen **odd one** with a mark (Fig. 2.9), as 11 is not 1 + 1 + 2, but = 3. As for the Arabian figures, 11 is not 1 + 1 = 2, but eleven.

Binary 10 is therefore marked   —x—   = 2
Binary 11 is therefore marked   —o—   = 3

Figure 2.9

The use of 'X' and 'O' thus indicates a carrying over of Yang force from the left column, as shown in Figure 2.10 on the next page. Whether or not the initial figures are drawn with change-marks, the left and right columns combine, contracting into one figure.

Figure 2.10:

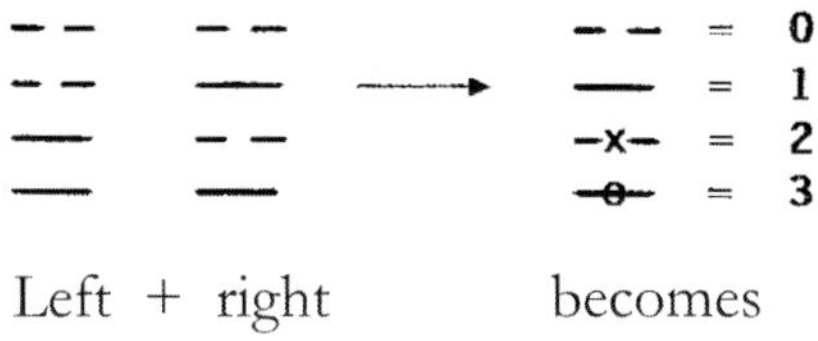

```
| |      | |              - -   =  0
| |      ---              ---   =  1
---      | |             -x-    =  2
---      ---             -o-    =  3

Left  +  right          becomes
```

A simple mathematical law makes clear exactly why these marked lines must be changing lines:

```
even  +  even  =  even
even  +  odd   =  odd
odd   +  even  =  odd
odd   +  odd   =  even
```

Binary numbers and their decimal values, expressed as lines (Fig. 2.11), show that what appears as one column really represents two columns:

Figure 2.11:

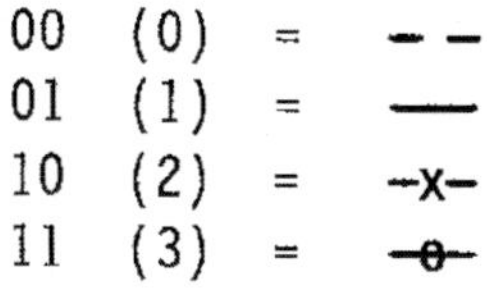

```
00  (0)  =  - -
01  (1)  =  ---
10  (2)  =  -x-
11  (3)  =  -o-
```

Thus, to **change** the lines actually means adding a third column (Fig. 2.12), derived from the left and right unmarked columns:

Figure 2.12:

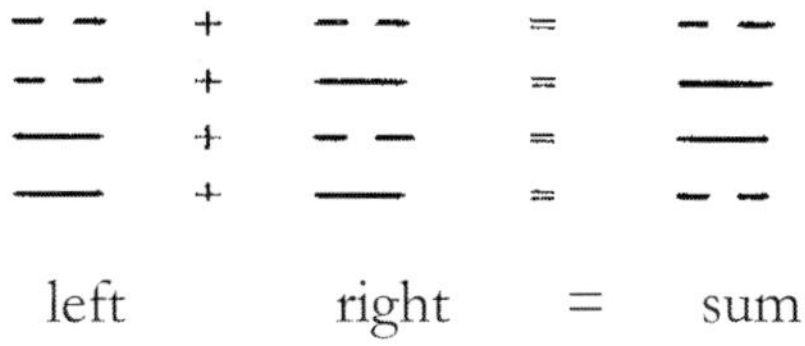

```
- -   +   - -   =   - -
- -   +   ---   =   ---
---   +   - -   =   ---
---   +   ---   =   - -

left      right   =   sum
```

Stated as the I Ching does, the invisible left column is contained in the right column, which then turns into an unmarked figure (Fig. 2.13).

Figure 2.13:

```
- -   =   - -
---   =   ---
-x-   =   ---
-o-   =   - -
```

19

In effect, I put the left column back in view. And since the columns are transposable, putting in the left column does not invalidate the law of odd and even. This simple principle can be easily shown (Fig. 2.14) in a circle:

odd   odd
   even

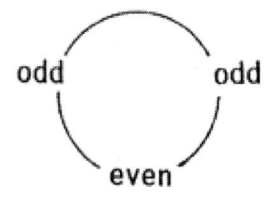

Figure 2.14

For reasons unknown, the I Ching keeps silent about this, as it is also silent on the third column. Nonetheless, I found confirmation of this principle within the branch of geomancy, whereby a randomly placed number of dots revealed the values of Yang and Yin.

Moreover, the third column can be surmised at a glance, which we shall see by using the numbers 2 and 3 to provide a mathematical extension of the concept of addition. In standard binary reasoning, we should omit 'X' and 'O' as they allow two lines to become four. But, as the marks suggest another logical system behind the binary system, we keep them in to symbolize the **flow** of Yang power through our **Time-line** circle.

To elaborate, when a Yang line is repeated, it constitutes a Yang force in motion, gathering momentum, thus intrinsically unstable and ready for change (odd + odd = even); so, the line is marked. This Yang-turned-into-Yin-line is not static; it continues having momentum, making it unstable; thus, a changing Yin line about to become another Yang line (odd + even = odd), and is so marked. Both changing lines are unstable, shown here with a picture of our magnified timeline (Fig. 2.15).

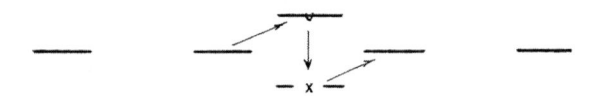

Figure 2.15

If we now place the three lines capable of change in a similar pattern as our odd/even circle, with the unchanging 00-value Yin line in the center, appropriately (Fig. 2.16), we see something curious. The natural flow from the lesser to greater values of the lines representing 1, 2 and 3, runs contrary to the following flow, where odd + odd = even, etc.

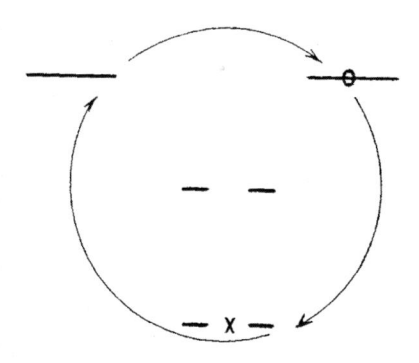

Figure 2.16

Returning to our time line and filling it arbitrarily with a Yang line ____ or a Yin line __ __, let us place six momentums together (Fig. 2.17) within one time quantum:

Figure 2.17

Let's view them separately from the rest of the timeline in a column (Fig. 2.18)

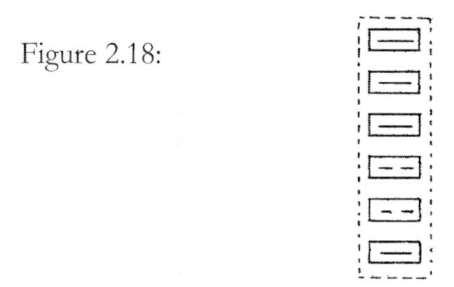

Figure 2.18:

With the timeline receded from view, we don't really know whether our quanta came in view by stepping up or stepping down, yet we may surmise that it happens alternately up and down, rhythmically.

Figure 2.19:

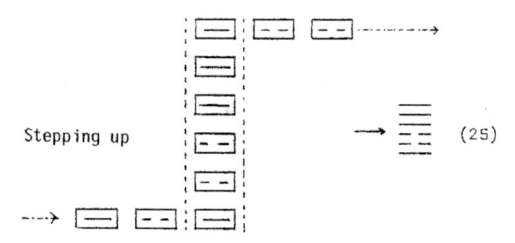

[figure showing stepping up to Hexagram (25)]

Stepping up, in this particular case (Fig. 2.19), signifies Hexagram 25. Of course, if the line was filled differently, another Hexagram would appear. If stepping down, (Fig. 2.20) this case becomes Hexagram 26.

Figure 2.20:

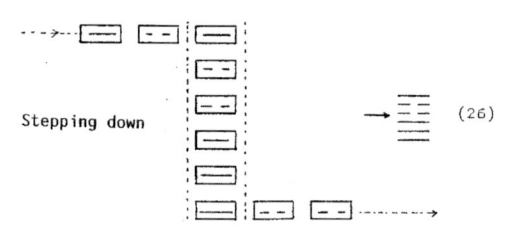

[figure showing stepping down to Hexagram (26)]

So, by stepping up and down with the same sequence of Yin and Yang lines (Fig. 2.21), we arrive at this picture of Hexagrams 25 and 26.

Figure 2.21

[figure showing Hexagrams 25 and 26]

These Hexagrams, in Binary form, are 100111 and 111001, which give us the Numerical Sums 39 and 57. Let's now fill in 6 Time-quanta with this same sequence of Yang and Yin lines stepping up, followed by 6 more Time-quanta in a random sequence by stepping down (Fig. 2.22).

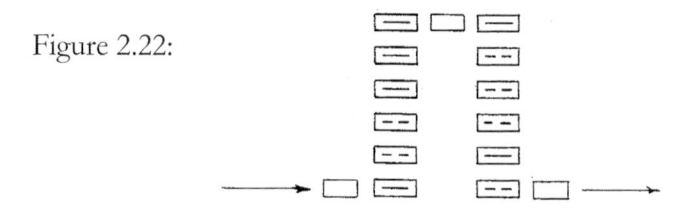

Figure 2.22:

[figure]

So we can now recognize the first and second time quanta, just shown, as Hexagrams 25 and 4. And if the time flow continues, stepping up through a third column of 6 moments compressed as a time quantum, it must obey the **law of odd and even**, and the third Hexagram formed can follow only one special line sequence; Hexagram 58, shown here:

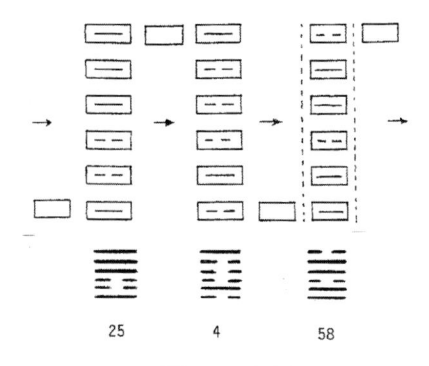

Figure 2.23

Putting these three Hexagrams in a circle (Fig. 2.24) shows how the law of odd and even works through, on all six levels, completing the cycle and working in either direction. These there Hexagrams together are a **Triole**. **Tri** stands for three and **ole** is short for Whole.

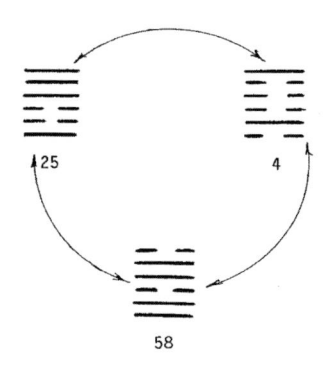

Figure 2.24

The law of odd and even makes it easy to see the changes. If a line is about to change, it receives a mark. If a Yang line is repeated, it always receives the mark 'O' in the middle.

A changing Yang line always becomes a changing Yin line, marked with 'X' in the middle. With the marks (Fig. 2.25), any one member of this Triole can represent the **whole**. It is three in one.

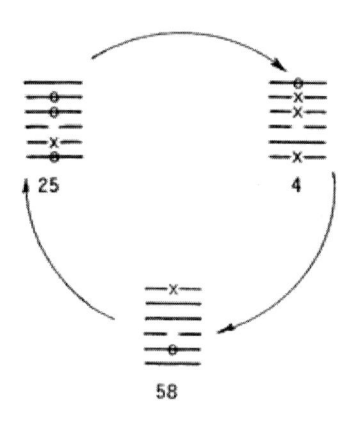

Figure 2.25

Thus, the principle of **change** is also one of **return**, is shown again in a circle wherein the flow circulates (Fig. 2.26). The first brings forth the second, which turns into the third change and, as it is a close circuit, the third returns to the first.

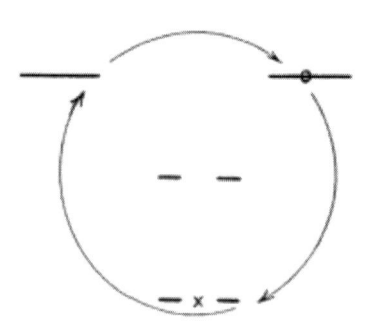

Figure 2.26

CHAPTER 3: TRIOLES

Upon examining an enlarged picture of our first Timeline (Fig. 3.1), something else becomes apparent.

Figure 3.1

The Timeline itself shows two faces; according to our disposition, we either see one moment of time as Yang ——— or focus upon the **un-time** between moments, forming a Yin — — image. Containing these images within the closed circles (Fig. 3.2) leads us to the very root of the **oracle**, which gradually correlated Yang and Yin principles with the concepts of good or bad decisions relating to happenings evolving in **Time**.

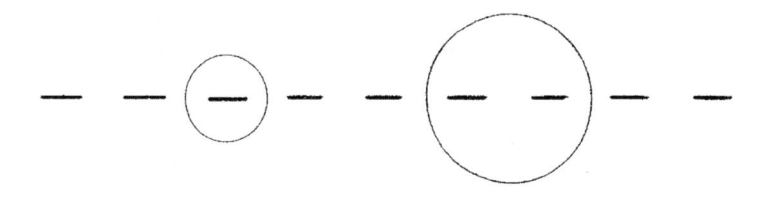

Figure 3.2

Very early in history, people tossed shells or coins for this purpose. The way the object landed decided **yes** or **no** for meaningful questions, such as "Do we go to war or not?" "Do we move from here or not?" The variations are endless. Even today, people often toss a coin to settle matters (Fig. 3.3), or determine a winner and a loser, and by agreement, people **obey** the oracle.

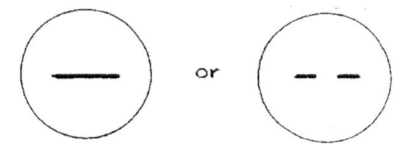

Figure 3.3

In old China, empty and filled circles (Fig. 3.4) were used to symbolize Yin and Yang. These white and black circles developed later into the strokes we know. The dichotomy had endless applications with only a dichromatic display.

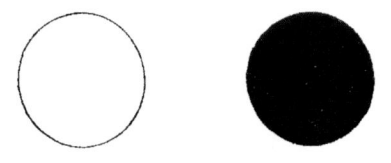

Figure 3.4

The circles were also filled with red and white, with the same meanings as we ascribe today, with red and green traffic lights. The practice of filling circles to decide an outcome is observed today too, as a way to answer multiple-choice tests, and ballot voting to pick a candidate to win a title or position. Since the circle symbolized time, and the two values were faces of unseen factors of time, the Chinese merged both into a universally recognized symbol (Fig. 3.5) of changing time:

Figure 3.5

The old form of the oracle continued to display a hexagram using the small circles, as in this case (Fig. 3.6), showing Hexagram 25.

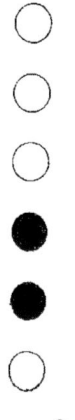

○
○
○
●
●
○

Figure 3.6

As long as one stays with only one coin, the answer is always a simple yes or no; in Chinese terms, Yang or Yin. Yet, this simple method becomes more complex, when translating into Yang or Yin. Even the Chinese, considered experts by most, disagree amongst themselves on various points, so the only really simple part of this form of divination is the coin tossing operation, which follows binary rules.

The Chinese undertook a more complicated step, which may be seen as the start of mathematics, while the figures remained heavily imbued with symbolic meanings. Supposing the ordinary man in 'old' China could count on his fingers or upon whatever was at hand, why would he bother with a system of only two values? The reason was and still is: decisions must be made, for which we cannot rely on the knowledge we already have or can gather. We ask 'The Gods' or 'Heaven' or 'The Forces' or 'The Ancients' – whatever we understand as an unseen, wiser guiding presence. In modern times, we may say we communicate with the 'unconscious.' But who can say what is the difference?

As soon as TWO coins are used, or one is used twice, then a step is made which we shall now discuss. The Chinese mark their lines vertically from the bottom upward. Westerners write numbers horizontally, with smaller values on the right, greater on the left. So, writing ____ ____ is equivalent to 0; and _____ = 1. And with the first four 'Elements,' which we earlier referred to as the four 'Bigrams,' the second place was understood as being mathematically important. The appearance, thus, of the 2 and the 3, is a subject on which the I Ching keeps silent, leaving us to guess if the sages developing this remarkable book knew about it.

It appears as the workable 'element' on the coins, and elementary, they are now named *Two and Three* (Fig. 3.7), and by most dedicated I Ching students who sit quietly and manipulate the yarrow stalks, throwing coins is considered too 'elementary.'

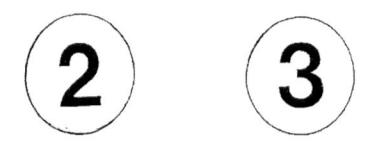

Figure 3.7

The four elements (Fig. 3.8) are:

Figure 3.8

In our binary 'place' system, we write 00, 01, 10, 11. In this way, it is not difficult to count further with only two values. Writing from left to right, or from bottom to top makes no difference. Some people write from right to left also. They all understand the same principle (Fig. 3.9), as already discussed.

$$00 = 0$$
$$01 = 1$$
$$10 = 2$$
$$11 = 3$$

Figure 3.9

As we have seen, the Chinese at some point of their history, introduced a compressed form of writing these numbers using the 'marks' as we know them, as shown in Figure 3.10 on the next page.

Figure 3.10:
```
00 = 0  =  ▬▬  ▬▬
01 = 1  =  ▬▬▬▬▬
10 = 2  =  ▬▬ X ▬▬
11 = 3  =  ▬▬ O ▬▬
```

It is easy to see the symbolic idea behind the choice of these particular marks, the 'O' and 'X'. The 'Eastern' symbol of Heaven is a wheel that 'turns' while the Earth, which was thought to keep still is symbolized by a circle holding steady (Fig. 3.11). We cannot blame the Chinese for their simplistic idea of the Universe, when we in the west did no better. This was their way of accentuating the ideas of 'fixedness' and 'change'.

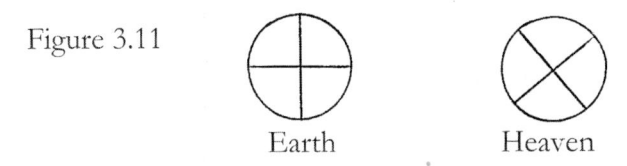

Figure 3.11

⊕ ⊗

Earth   Heaven

The 'fixed' way of the oracle was only Naught ▬▬ ▬▬ and One ▬▬▬▬▬ respectively. The 'changing' way of the oracle involved Two and Three also. Writing it from the bottom upward gives us a clue of the difference, shown here below, Figure 3.12:

```
Heavenly:   11 = 3  =  ▬▬ O ▬▬
            10 = 2  =  ▬▬ X ▬▬
            - - - - - - - - - -
Earthly:    01 = 1  =  ▬▬▬▬▬
            00 = 0  =  ▬▬  ▬▬
```

The legendary Sage, Fu His, using a binary system, developed the hexagrams without marks. The philosophers behind it kept silent on the 'Quaternary' system, which is clearly involved if using marks. The 2 and 3 represent the faces of the coin and the 'head and tail' of the oracle, which reminds us of the tortoise.

Using the numbers 2 and 3 for a formula also gives the distances of the planets from the Sun in astronomical units, more accurately than the familiar Law of Titius-Bode.

If 0 and 1 are the only values used, then the system is complete with 64 images and is fairly easy to handle. The Triole system requires 4096 images (64²) to be complete, making it fairly complex, and a difficult task to devise a textbook with so many interrelated explanations.

Yet, employing the change with 'marks' already does it, by drawing a second hexagram and culling symbolic information from both. Some people become really expert at it. The possibilities are 64 x 64 = 4096 combinations, which I call 'The Greater Heaven', symbolized by the well-known T'ai Chi symbol (Fig. 3.13) wherein the 'marks' appear as white and black dots.

Figure 3.13

The Moon was universally used to symbolize changes on Earth and the natural choice of 64 images of 6 lines each = 384 lines, which is about 13 synodic moon periods (13 x 29.5 = 383.4 days) relating to 'earthly changes' and 'The Smaller Heaven.' Thus, with only 64 Hexagrams, we are symbolically on Earth, working with earthly problems.

With 4096 images, we expand beyond, into 'The Greater Heaven' – the spheres of the planetary influences. And the two and three can be used to compute their distances from the Sun.

Within the great 'cubic' of 64 x 64 x 64, symbolizing the 'Stars' or whole universe, which I call 'The Utmost Heaven', Trioles form a symbolic Tetrahedron to help us understand the workings of the Greater Heaven, as depicted in Figure 3.14. 'Marks' are essential to enter the complexity of this expanded concept of the Yang and Yin forces.

Figure 3.14

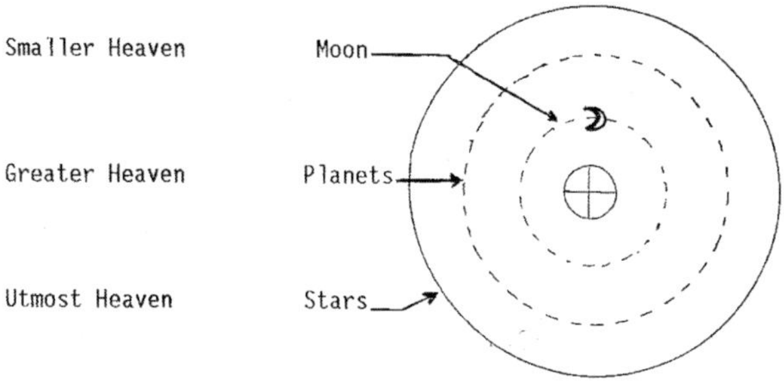
Smaller Heaven
Moon
Greater Heaven
Planets
Utmost Heaven
Stars

As the numbering of 4096 Trioles follows base 4 rules, a Quaternary system, the four signs are written as follows, in the order 0 - 1 - 2 - 3.

Figure 3.15

Counting through six levels, starting at the bottom and moving upward:

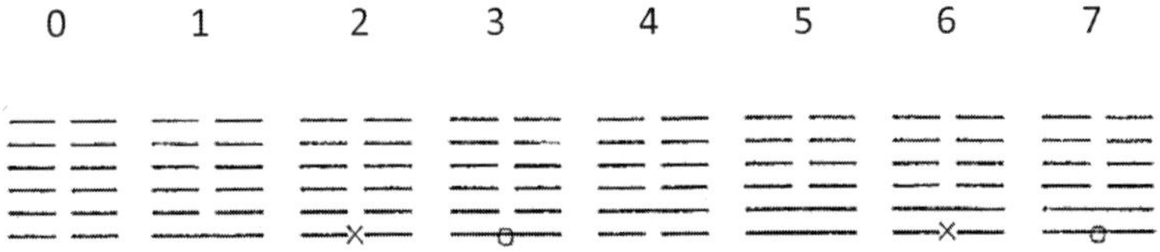
0
1
2
3
4
5
6
7

Figure 3.16

Each image identified by a number also represents a Triole. Every Hexagram appears in the list 64 times, each marked differently. For example, we can show Hexagrams 129 and 1792 separately as follows:

Figure 3.17:

129
1792

Or we can show the Triole each image represents: Figure 3.18:

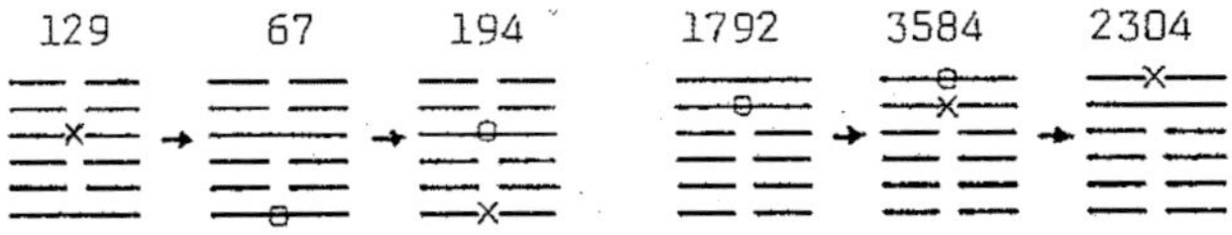
129
67
194
1792
3584
2304

To list 4096 possible Trioles, of course, involves repetitions, as each circular pattern appears in three forms of the same images. While numbering the Hexagrams from 1 to 4095, based on their Quaternary mathematical progression, I divided by 3 (4095/3 = 1365), handling them as 1365 Trioles to avoid a repetitive list. Sorting them out from the beginning, a peculiar pattern emerged which may serve as an aid to check the text in the I Ching. The 1365 Trioles organize into six groups:

Group 0	1/3 Triole
Group 1	1 Triole
Group 2	4 Trioles
Group 3	16 Trioles
Group 4	64 Trioles
Group 5	256 Trioles
Group 6	1024 Trioles

Within these groupings, interesting figures emerge.

Group 0: Because 0 only repeats itself, it = 1/3 Triole.

Group 1:   Triole 1…3…2 is the first to contain the other two;
           Triole 2…1…3 and
           Triole 3…2…1 ("…" = "becomes").

Notice the order:

Triole 0 =	0…0…0
Triole 1 =	1…3…2
Triole 2 =	2…1…3
Triole 3 =	3…2…1

As Trioles 2 and 3 merely reorder Triole 1, they can be left out. Groups 0 and 1 together form a basic pattern, recognizable throughout the whole sequence, which we'll call a 'Cell'.

Group 0:	0…0…0
Group 1:	1…3…2 Cell
	2…1…3
	3…2…1

If the top number of each column = "x", three patterns emerge.

Analyzing the left column:

$$x = 0 \text{ and } x + 0 = 0$$
$$+ 1 = 1 \quad \text{Pattern 1}$$
$$+ 2 = 2$$
$$+ 3 = 3$$

Analyzing the middle column:

$$x = 0 \text{ and } x + 0 = 0$$
$$+ 3 = 3 \quad \text{Pattern 2}$$
$$+ 1 = 1$$
$$+ 2 = 2$$

Analyzing the right column:

$$x = 0 \text{ and } x + 0 = 0$$
$$+ 2 = 2 \quad \text{Pattern 3}$$
$$+ 3 = 3$$
$$+ 1 = 1$$

While the numbers grow bigger, we continue adding x to our basic 'Cell' numbers, where x = the top number of each column.

Group 2:   4…12…8
           5…15…10
           6…13…11
           7…14…9

Group 2 follows the basic pattern; the left column numbers increase in sequence from 4 to 7.

Analyzing the left column:

$$x = 4 \text{ and } x + 0 = 4$$
$$+ 1 = 5 \quad \text{Pattern 1}$$
$$+ 2 = 6$$
$$+ 3 = 7$$

Analyzing the middle column:

$$x = 12 \text{ and } x + 0 = 12$$
$$+ 3 = 15 \quad \text{Pattern 2}$$
$$+ 1 = 13$$
$$+ 2 = 14$$

Analyzing the right column:

$$x = 8 \text{ and } x + 0 = 8$$
$$+ 2 = 10 \quad \text{Pattern 3}$$
$$+ 3 = 11$$
$$+ 1 = 9$$

Group 3 has 16 Trioles, beginning with numbers 16 to 31, forming four Cells:

Group 3:

16…48…32
17…51…34   Cell 0
18…49…35
19…50…33

20…60…40
21…63…42   Cell 1
22…61…43
23…62…41

24…52…44
25…55…46   Cell 2
26…53…47
27…54…45

28…56…36
29…59…38   Cell 3
30…57…39
31…58…37

Note: The top row, 16…48…32, forms a '1…3…2 rule' consistent with the first row of the first Cell of each Group. In each Cell, the left column follows pattern 1; the middle column, pattern 2 and the right column, pattern 3.

The middle column, pattern 2, is: $x + 0, + 3, + 1, + 2$.

So, Group 3 starts with $x = 48$:

$$x + 0 = 48 \quad \text{in Cell 0}$$
$$+ 3 = 51$$
$$+ 1 = 49$$
$$+ 2 = 50$$

And continues with x = 52:

x + 0	= 52	
+ 3	= 55	in Cell 2
+ 1	= 53	
+ 2	= 54	

Then continues with x = 56:

x + 0	= 56	
+ 3	= 59	in Cell 3
+ 1	= 57	
+ 2	= 58	

And concludes with x = 60:

x + 0	= 60	
+ 3	= 63	in Cell 1
+ 1	= 61	
+ 2	= 62	

Column 3 of Cell 0 must start with 32, following the '1…3…2 rule' discussed earlier, and in this case, 1 = 16.

The right column of Group 3 Trioles, 32 through 47, follows the basic pattern 3 from Cell to Cell: x + 0, + 2, + 3, + 1.

So, Group 3 starts with x = 32:

x + 0	= 32	
+ 2	= 34	in Cell 0
+ 3	= 35	
+ 1	= 33	

And continues with x = 36:

x + 0	= 36	
+ 2	= 38	in Cell 3
+ 3	= 39	
+ 1	= 37	

Then continues with x = 40:

x + 0	= 40	
+ 2	= 42	in Cell 1
+ 3	= 43	
+ 1	= 41	

And concludes with x = 44:

x + 0	= 44	
+ 2	= 46	in Cell 2
+ 3	= 47	
+ 1	= 45	

CHAPTER 4: HEARING THE ORACLE

To avoid confusion while discussing so many kinds of numbers, we'll use this key: When referring to a Hexagram, we'll write 'H' before the number. For Binary numbers, we'll write 'B'; Trioles will be preceded by 'T'; Line numbers, 'L'.

Our example of the Group 3 Trioles is a short list compared to the Trioles in the other groups. To find the Binary equivalent of any Hexagram (Fig. 4.1):

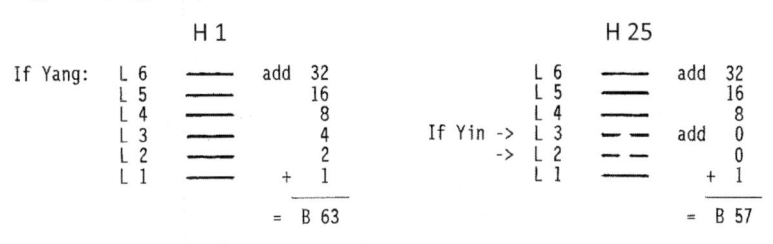

```
              H 1                              H 25
If Yang:  L 6 ——  add 32                  L 6 ——  add 32
          L 5 ——      16                  L 5 ——      16
          L 4 ——       8                  L 4 ——       8
          L 3 ——       4    If Yin ->  L 3 – –  add  0
          L 2 ——       2           ->  L 2 – –       0
          L 1 ——    +  1                  L 1 ——   +  1
                    ——————                          ——————
                  = B 63                          = B 57
```

Figure 4.1

To determine from a Binary number, which lines belong to the Hexagram image, reverse the calculation, beginning with L 6:

If 32 can be subtracted from the Binary number, L 6 is Yang.
If 32 cannot be subtracted, L 6 is Yin.
If 16 can be subtracted from the remainder, L 5 is Yang.
If not, L 5 is Yin.
Continue the process, subtracting   8 to determine L4,
                                    4 to determine L3,
                                    2 to determine L 2
                             and   1 to determine L 1.

Each time you can subtract a line's number value, the line is Yang.

If not, you know the line is Yin, and you can then continue subtracting with the next smaller line value.

For example (Fig. 4.2), using B 36:

```
36 - 32 is possible; L 6 is Yang             L 6  ———
Remainder 4 - 16 not possible; L 5 is Yin    L 5  — —
4 - 8 not possible; L 4 is also Yin          L 4  — —
4 - 4 possible; L 3 is Yang                  L 3  ———
0 - 2 not possible; L 2 is Yin               L 2  — —
0 - 1 not possible; L 1 is Yin               L 1  — —
```

Figure 4.2

Unfortunately, at present, we have no method with which to derive the Hexagram number. For this, the I Ching provides a useful matrix of upper Trigrams shown at the top, and lower Trigrams shown on the left side to aid students. In our example, B 36 = H 52. To find the Triole number of a given Hexagram, the first Key (Fig. 4.3) is:

```
— —      yin           = 0
———      yang          = 1
—X—      yin-change    = 2
—O—      yang-change   = 3
```

Figure 4.3

The second Key (Fig. 4.4) is:

		— —	———	—X—	—O—
Level	6	0	1024	2048	3072
"	5	0	256	512	768
"	4	0	64	128	192
"	3	0	16	32	48
"	2	0	4	8	12
"	1	0	1	2	3
Column		1	2	3	4

Figure 4.4

These two keys suffice to derive the Triole number from a Hexagram image, and vice versa. This Quaternary operation, like the Binary, starts with L 6, at the top level.

An example (Fig. 4.5), reading in the second Key:

```
—x—     Third Column      2048    6th Level
———     Second    "        256    5th    "
—o—     Fourth    "        192    4th    "
—o—     Fourth    "         48    3rd    "
— —     First     "          0    2nd    "
———     Second    "          1    1st    "
                 ─────────────
              = Triole  2545
```

Figure 4.5

To convert a Triole number back to a Hexagram image, we follow a similar method as with Binary, but with the Quaternary counting:

Subtract the highest number on Level 6 from the Triole number; if impossible, try each next lower number until no more are possible. Whenever subtraction is possible, the line is the same as that at the top of the column. If on a particular level no number can be subtracted, the line is Yin. For example (Fig. 4.6), Triole 376:

```
Level 6 numbers are higher than 376;   L 6 = Yin        — —
subtract 376 - 256 (2nd column);       L 5 = Yang       ———
120 remains; 120 - 64 (3rd column);    L 4 = Yang       ———
56 left, 56 - 48 (4th column); L 3 = changing Yang      —o—
8 left, 8 - 8 (3rd column);    L 2 = changing Yin       —x—
0 left;                                L 1 = Yin        — —
```

Figure 4.6

The I Ching trigrams matrix shows this to be Hexagram 31. Being 'marked', the normal procedure is to derive from this a second image (Fig. 4.7), which becomes Hexagram 47.

Figure 4.7

As marked Hexagrams belong in a Quaternary system, we derive our 3rd Hexagram from the 2nd (Fig. 4.8) by retaining the appropriate marks:

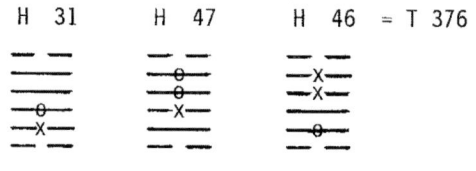

H 31   H 47   H 46 = T 376

Figure 4.8

Many beautifully conceived interpretations of the I Ching Lines have been written, with numerous translations, which are read along with the Hexagram's 'Image' and 'Judgment'. We may consider the meanings of each marked line, or simply let the number of marks determine which line to read. Marks imply the Hexagram's 'moving power', with the number of Yang lines being its strengths. Reading the Lines of Trioles may require slightly altering the meanings.

As an example, let's use a high number. For Triole 2395 (Fig. 4.9), we:

```
Subtract 2048 (3rd column); level 6    =   —x—
deduct    256 (2nd column); level 5    =   ———
deduct     64 (2nd column); level 4    =   ———
deduct     16 (2nd column); level 3    =   ———
deduct      8 (3rd column); level 2    =   —x—
deduct      3 (4th column); level 1    =   —o—
```

Figure 4.9

This is shown to be Hexagram 49 with three marks. As a Triole (Fig. 4.10), it works out as 49…44…41.

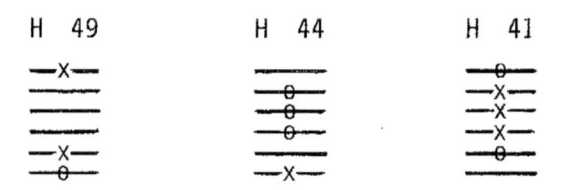

H 49   H 44   H 41

Figure 4.10

This example was associated with the question, "What is the best course to take?" pertaining to a meeting which had to be arranged. According to the translation of Roderic and Amy Max Sorrell, these Hexagrams (Fig. 4.11) are named:

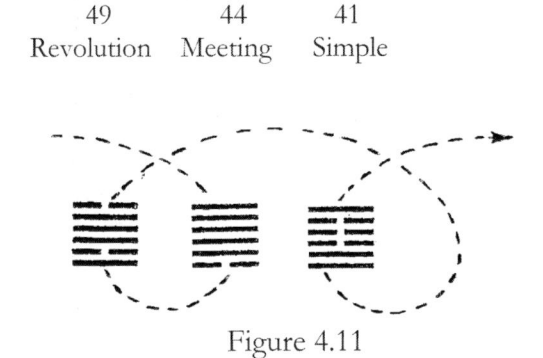

         49   44   41
   Revolution Meeting Simple

Figure 4.11

According to the same version, the lines are:

H 49 (3) "When it is discussed three times, people will trust it."
This means important change can only happen with others' support.

H 44 (4) "No fish in the bag, misfortune."
This warns that no material gain is involved, symbolized by 'fish'.

H 41 (5) "Cannot refuse a gift of a valuable tortoise shell"

The gift is the sound spiritual advice of the I Ching itself. As Roderic's version says, 'You have nothing to give and nothing for yourself'. Thus, there need not be an exchange of the usual obligatory sort. Accepting this advice, the meeting was postponed until the conditions of the first Hexagram were met, whereby the support of others was secured. Below is our example, returning to the 'first' Hexagram: (Fig. 4.12)

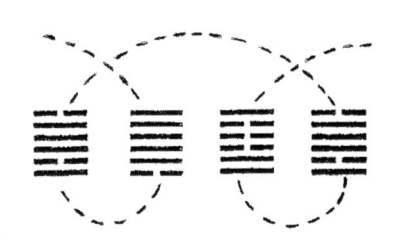

Figure 4.12:

Returning to the first Hexagram in the fourth place reflects the idea of time as a cyclic flow, wherein recognizable moments of compressed time-quanta are made visible as the jumps which Time makes through Un-time. On a universal scale, all Trioles mark and meaningfully symbolize three points of a circle of experience (Fig. 4.13), where each beginning is also an ending:

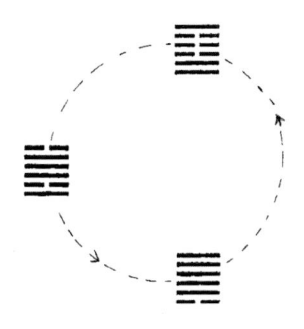

Figure 4.13

This Triole begins with 'Revolution' being initiated and upon return, completed, whereby one immediately experiences a strong impulse to start an enterprise or go somewhere again.

The second point of this Triole involves a 'Meeting', which has strong overtones of meeting a partner (which may mean sexual involvement) and is appropriate for encountering one's opposite.

The Triole's third point is 'Decrease' or in Roderic's version, 'Simple'. Reflecting the idea that going away from the meeting point simplifies things, favoring a return to the beginning state (Fig. 4.14).

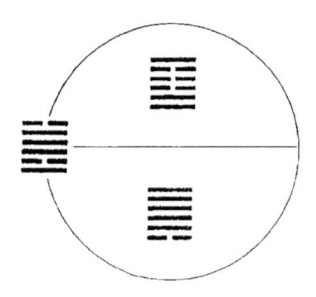

Figure 4.14

It is symbolic that just this oracle gives such understanding of the cyclic process. Revolution is the only Hexagram to also bear the connotation of 'Change', (see Thomas Cleary's The Buddhist I Ching), as our revolving Earth is a good example of a 'Revolution' bringing a certain point – or planet – back to its beginning.

Actually, this point of reference of Earth revolving around the Sun in a spiraling movement against a starry background (Fig 4.15), gives us our standard measures of time. And, just as our experience of physical weight is altered in space, as we distance ourselves from the pull of Earth's gravity, so our recognition of time is altered as our consciousness expands beyond the weighty, Earthly matters, to the brighter spheres of 'Utmost Heaven'.

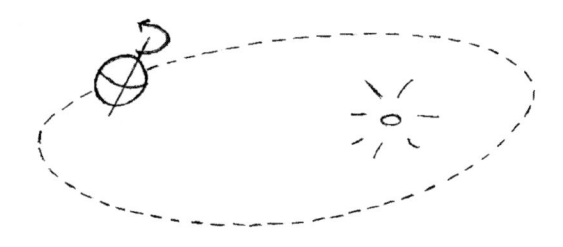

Figure 4.15

Time, and our Timeline, was recognized as a circle early in history. Traditionally the Hexagrams were shown using circular patterns, and many other cases exist of people showing this principle; our clock, our calendars and the many oracle systems, which also place their symbols in a circular pattern. Each demonstrates an understanding of our experience of time as circular (Fig. 4.16), where each revolution is one part of a continuously coiling spiral.

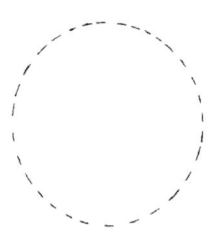

Figure 4.16

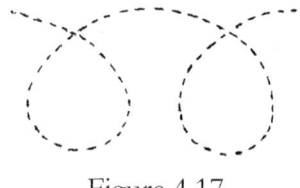

Figure 4.17

Figure 4.17 above, shows this spiral coiling along an imaginary line. If we visualize the 'loops' as 'pockets' of experience (Fig. 4.18), we can recognize herein a Yang force.

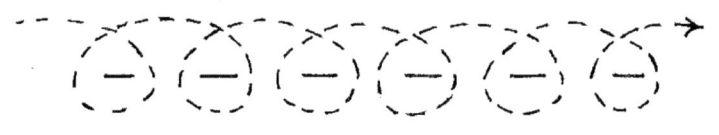

Figure 4.18

The closed loops of Time, like 'tears' from the eye of the Bodhisattva (Fig. 4.19), convey our incarnational struggles:

Figure 4.19

The open space of the 'jump' across Un-time (Fig. 4.20), forming unseen bridges between experiences, aptly symbolizes and reflects a Yin force:

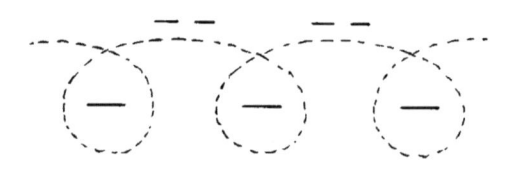

Figure 4.20

Using the idea of a spiral with an earlier example in this chapter, we see that the 'normal' way of drawing a Hexagram and from that, another (Fig. 4.21), embraces exactly one 'pocket' of experience:

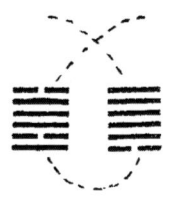

Figure 4.21

By drawing a Quaternary model, a second 'time pocket' is embraced (Fig. 4.22), and the function of the Yin force can be visualized. Notice how the spiraling flow of Time seems to pass through the 'returning Hexagram' the opposite way of the first. Of course, the direction is the same, but experienced differently, just as Earth continues revolving on its axis in the same direction, though we alternately experience day and night, then day and so forth.

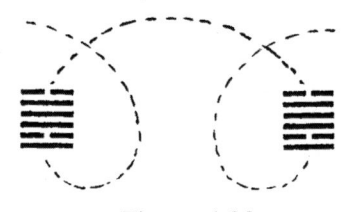

Figure 4.22

The 2nd and 3rd Triole members on this spiral image 'jump' across the 'gap' of Yin (fig. 4.23). It is indeed extraordinary, how this 3rd Hexagram – this jump across the un-known – has been, UN-known until now to the general reader. To understand it requires 'squaring' your base of two and thinking mathematically – *and metaphorically* – in a higher dimension.

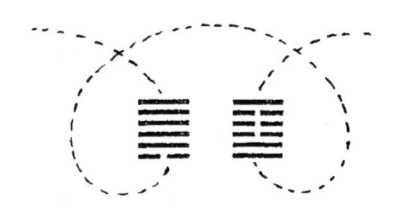

Figure 4.23

To use a Triole for guidance on a question, the method of counting the number of marks and reading just that line can be less confusing than reading text for many oracle changes indicated by all the marked lines, which can be somewhat disturbing. In our example below, H 49 has 3 marks, so we read the text for "Nine on the third place" though Line 3 of our H 49 image is unmarked. H 44 has 4 marks, so we read the text for "Nine in the fourth place," coinciding with the actual image. H 41 has 5 changes, so we read "Six in the fifth place," also coinciding with the image.

                Revolution   Meeting   Simple

Read: line 3 +   line 4 +   line 5

Figure 4.24

Usually, the oracle's three lines fit together fairly well. If the meanings seem a bit dim, you can adjust by viewing the Hexagram in the light of an inter-relating structure, as proposed below, with the quaternary approach. This involves understanding how the 64 Hexagrams relate to each other, with the added knowledge of the Trioles. Of course, all other methods in the I Ching apply to a Triole as well. You can even separate them and read them as if you had made 3 oracles the 'usual' way (Fig. 4.25), where marked lines appear only in the first Hexagram.

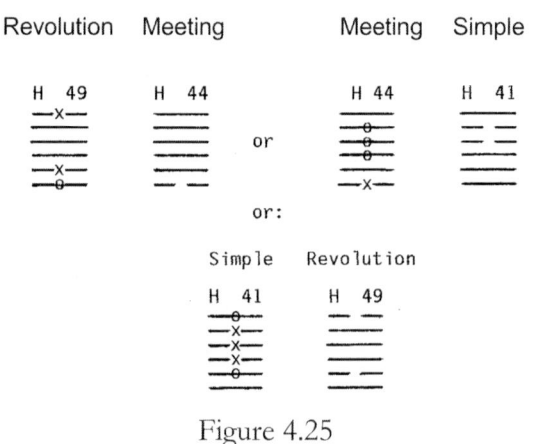

Revolution Meeting   Meeting Simple

or:

Simple Revolution

Figure 4.25

Continuing the Time-spiral for our example, T 2395, we notice that the coil, by repetition of the Triole (Fig. 4.26), appears to flow through the images with an 'opposite flow': down H 44, up H 49, jumping two images to flow down H 49 and up H 41, then jumping two images to flow down H 41 and up H 44:

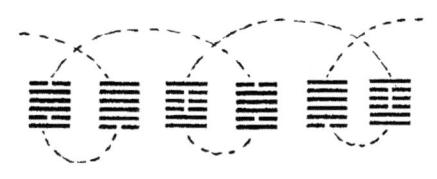

Figure 4.26

Clearly, our representation of a Timeline differs from what is normally thought of as the 'real' flow of Time. Our Timeline symbolizes the psychological impact of Time on humanity. This seemingly 'opposite flow' is inherently logical in **Psychological Time,** where the future rests in imagination's seeds, and the past is preserved in memory.

Figure 4.27

Continuing the sequence of T 2395 (Fig. 4.27), above, brings into view the two other, related Trioles. At what place this series starts on this coil, we cannot know and perhaps need not know. We will elaborate on this 'inner' movement later. Placing our example again on a smaller Time-circle (Fig. 4.28), we can see how these three Trioles are really one, separately expressed.

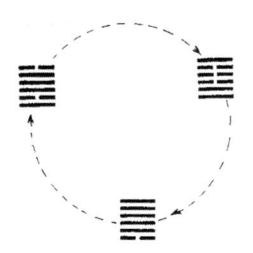

Figure 4.28

THE GIFT OF THE TORTOISE: NEW INSIGHTS INTO THE I CHING

CHAPTER 5: PATTERNS

The I Ching gives us 64 images, and still today, no one knows by what method (algorithm) the numbers are attached to a particular Hexagram. Everyone, especially the beginning student, has only recourse to a square ordering of the Hexagrams, with 'tri-grams' above and to the left of the square (Fig. 5.1) as a key to the number.

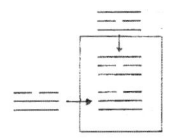

Figure 5.1

The way the trigrams are arranged outside the square determines how the inside of the square is ordered (Fig. 5.2).

2	23	8	20	16	35	45	12
15	52	39	53	62	56	31	33
7	4	29	59	40	64	47	6
46	18	48	57	32	50	28	44
24	27	3	42	51	21	17	25
36	22	63	37	55	30	49	13
19	41	60	61	54	38	58	10
11	26	5	9	34	14	43	1

Figure 5.2

Most of the time, the trigrams follow a Binary order, but curiously enough, two versions are shown; from the bottom level upward or the top level downward. For finding the number it would not make a difference. It does make a difference, however, for those who want to

49

go deeper into the material. The two versions depend on the way the Binary sequence is 'read'.

Most of the time they are also read from right to left. According to Shao Yung (Fig. 5.3):

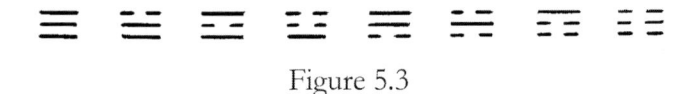

☰ ☱ ☲ ☳ ☴ ☵ ☶ ☷

Figure 5.3

According to Fu Hsi (Fig. 5.4):

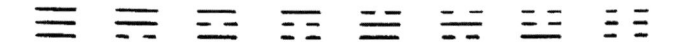

☰ ☱ ☲ ☳ ☴ ☵ ☶ ☷

Figure 5.4

We will call the square shown in Fig. 5.2 the 'Standard' to distinguish it from other versions. It is often displayed as a circle of Hexagrams (Fig. 5.5) symbolizing the Earth within the 'Smaller Heaven'.

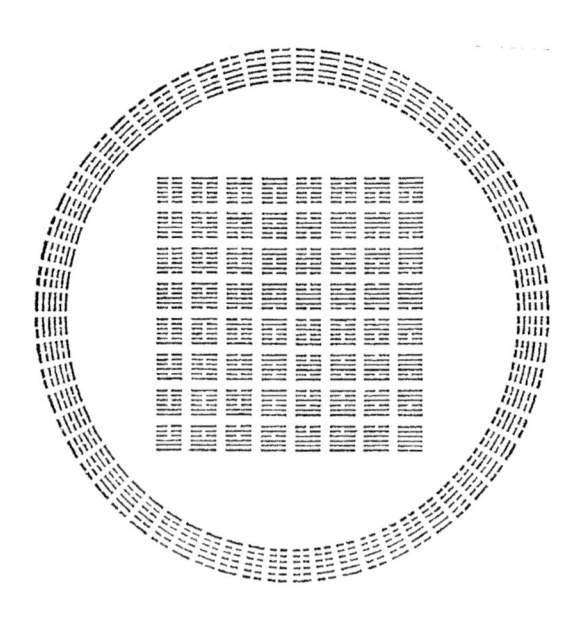

Figure 5.5

As the Smaller Heaven is symbolical of the pathway of the Moon, the phases of waxing and waning were important points to mark around the circle, shown below (Fig. 5.6) by the spiraling shadow. Quite naturally, they were associated with the eight Trigrams.

Figure 5.6

Just as the Moon's phases are the 'key' to growth patterns on Earth, the eight trigrams are a key into the number system of its symbolic representation. There is a lot to analyze, as this 'key' has a theoretical possibility of 8! Fortunately, we can state a few requirements, such as having the first trigram contain three Yang lines and the last trigram three Yin lines. That leaves us six trigrams (Fig. 5.7) to order and obtain a square different from the standard model.

Daughters   Sons

Figure 5.7

The naming of these six trigrams **sons** and **daughters** is beautifully symbolic, expressing **growth** and the **change** involved. The special Hexagram arrangement credited to King Wen shows 'pairs' which are either opposite or inverted to one another. Which one of the pair has a priority is not known.

If we set our square pattern on its corner-point and select pairs of opposites, (Fig. 5.8), their numbering can suggest a direction.

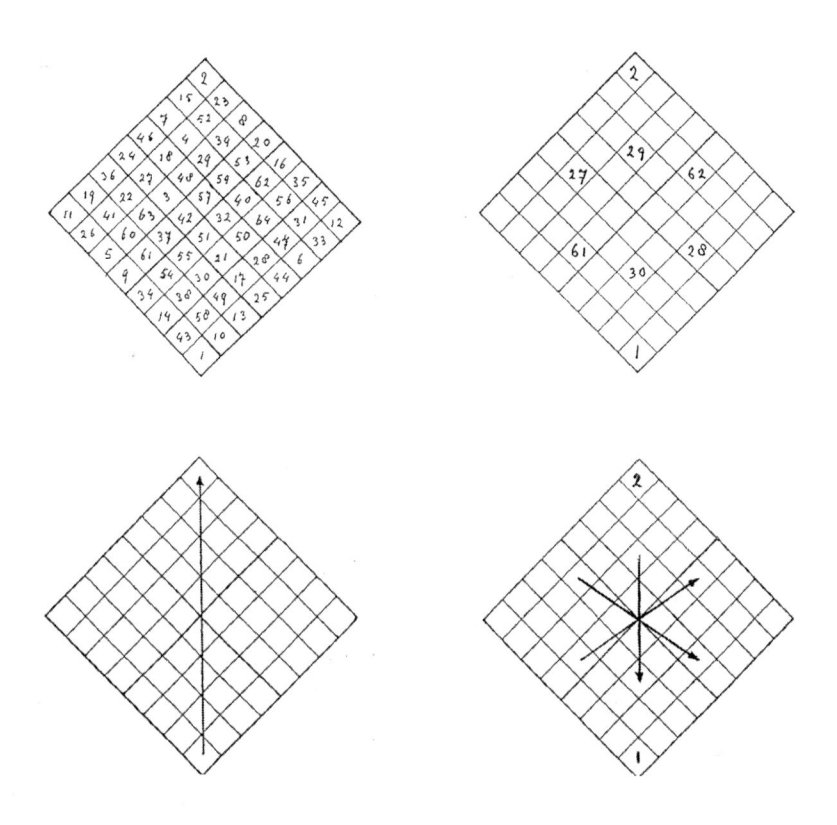

Figure 5.8

In such a way, we discover several interesting features of the internal organization. If the arrows suggest a movement of force, it would be more satisfying to have the arrow between 61 and 62 point the other way; since the force of H 1 is directed to H 2, toward the 'top', the 'center start' would then give force downward.

If we take the star pattern out of the square and place the Hexagrams on the star (Fig. 5.9), we notice that they do have a special relationship with one another. Four Trioles are discernable, and if we reverse the flow of odd and even, there are eight Trioles altogether.

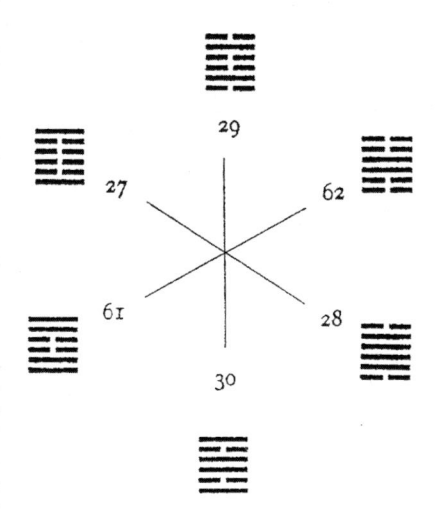

THE GIFT OF THE TORTOISE: NEW INSIGHTS INTO THE I CHING

Figure 5.9

In this pattern, the basic Triole is H 30…27…62. We can ignore the Triole number for the moment and focus on the other Trioles:

$$H\ 61…30…28$$
$$H\ 61…27…29$$
$$H\ 29…62…28$$

If the flow is reversed, they imply:

$$H\ 27…30…62$$
$$H\ 30…61…28$$
$$H\ 27…61…29$$
$$H\ 62…29…28$$

An interesting note: when checking their binary equivalences, we find two Trioles, 61…30…28 and 27…30…62, are special cases, as they do not add two terms to a third. In the other cases, adding the Binary numbers of two Triole members (subtracting 63 as superfluous) equals the Binary number of the third Hexagram of the Triole.

The Binary numbers are: H 27 = B 33
H 28 = B 30
H 29 = B 18
H 30 = B 45
H 61 = B 51
H 62 = B 12

Hexagram 1 and 2 (whose Binary equivalences are 63 and 0) seem aptly numbered. The flow goes from the active pole to the passive. If we put Hexagram 1 in the center of the star (Fig. 5.10), then the opposites around the circle are resolved into three Trioles across the center:

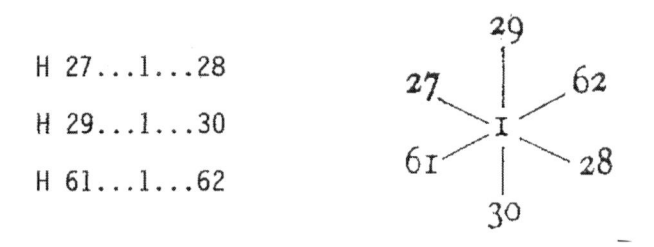

```
H 27...1...28
H 29...1...30
H 61...1...62
```

```
      29
  27    62
     I
  61    28
      30
```

Figure 5.10

Hexagram 1, combined with another Hexagram, creates the opposite Hexagram in every case. Combining H 2 with any Hexagram always creates, with the odd and even flow, the same Hexagram.

Other relationships follow a 'negative' logic, which we will discuss later. For now, we will keep our attention on the other places in the square. Finding a third Hexagram to complete a Triole with the other pairs, we see the following seven series (Fig. 5.11), with the third always being one of the self-inverting Hexagrams from our 'star' pattern:

H 1	H 27	H 28
H 11...12	H 23...24	H 25...26
17...18	43...44	37...38
53...54	55...56	39...40
63...64	59...60	45...46

H 29	H 30	H 61	H 62
H 7... 8	H 5... 6	H 3... 4	H 9...10
13...14	35...36	19...20	15...16
31...32	51...52	33...34	21...22
41...42	57...58	49...50	47...48

Figure 5.11

Putting every 'directional line' between the pairs in the square produces a picture (Fig. 5.12) that shows that the Textual order attributed to King Wen is not chaotic; nor is it easy to see where, if anywhere in the pattern, some pairs could be better placed:

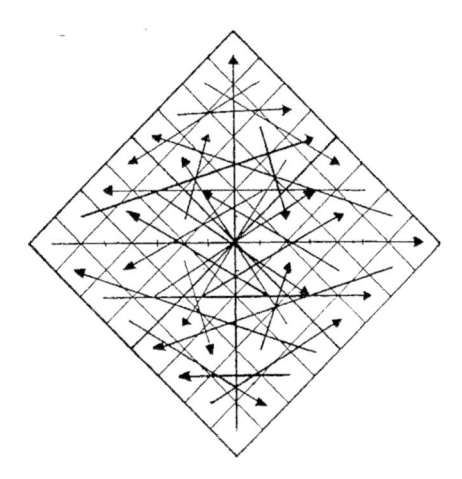

Figure 5.12

Placing only one of the series we made with a third Hexagram in the square (Figures 5.13 – 5.19) gives a clearer picture. We will look first at the group of Hexagram pairs, which are both the Yin/Yang conversion, and up/down inversion of one another:

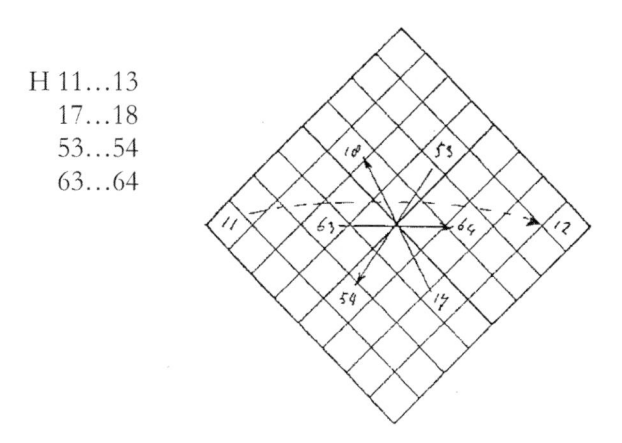

H 11…13
17…18
53…54
63…64

Figure 5.13

H 7... 8
 13...14
 31...32
 41...42

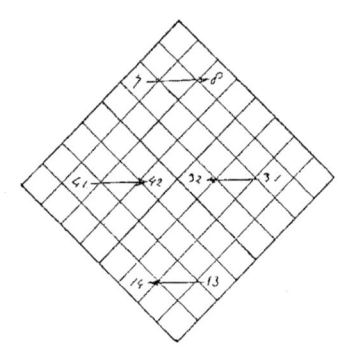

Figure 5.14

H 9...10
 15...16
 21...22
 47...48

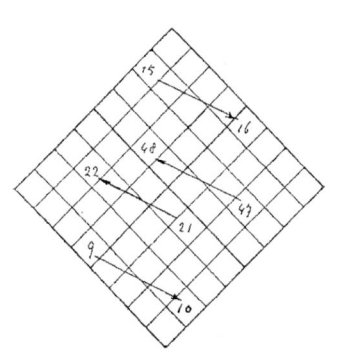

Figure 5.15

H 23...24
 43...44
 55...56
 59...60

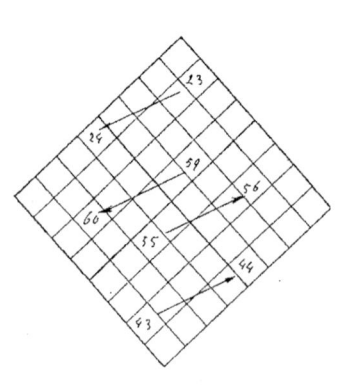

Figure 5.16

H 5 ... 6
　35...36
　51...52
　57...58

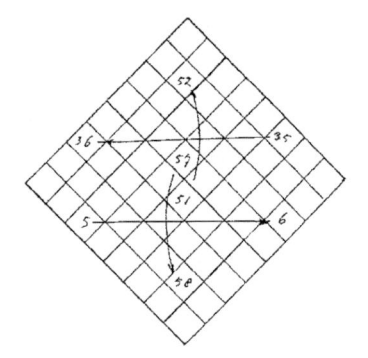

Figure 5.17

H 3 ... 4
　19...20
　33...34
　49...50

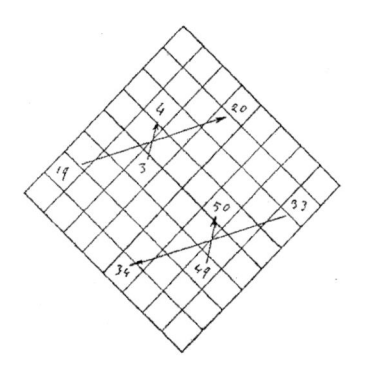

Figure 5.18

H 25...26
　37...38
　39...40
　45...46

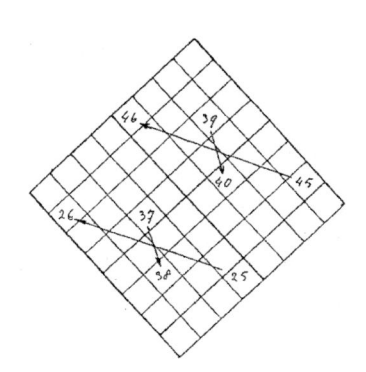

Figure 5.19

While these patterns in the square show an admirable organization of the numbers, some arrows' directions raise questions pointing to the need for a way to view the square as a more meaningful 'whole', as symbolic of the Earth's plane. Many other arrangements are possible, but regardless of what pattern you follow, a few arrows will always somehow not satisfy. This has led many researchers to believe that some of the pairs ought to be changed.

Following the argument, this square provides (Fig. 5.20) another example:

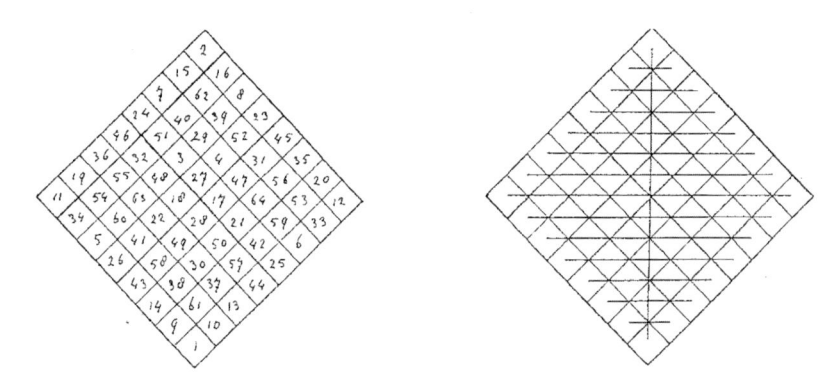

Figure 5.20

The Trigrams for the left side of this arrangement (Fig. 5.21) are:

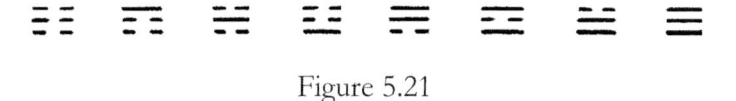

Figure 5.21

The Trigrams from the top downward to the right (Fig. 5.22) are:

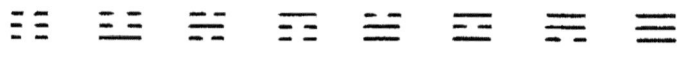

Figure 5.22

THE GIFT OF THE TORTOISE: NEW INSIGHTS INTO THE I CHING

Within this alternative square, we can draw arrow patterns (Figures 5.23 – 5.30) which, again, show peculiar features.

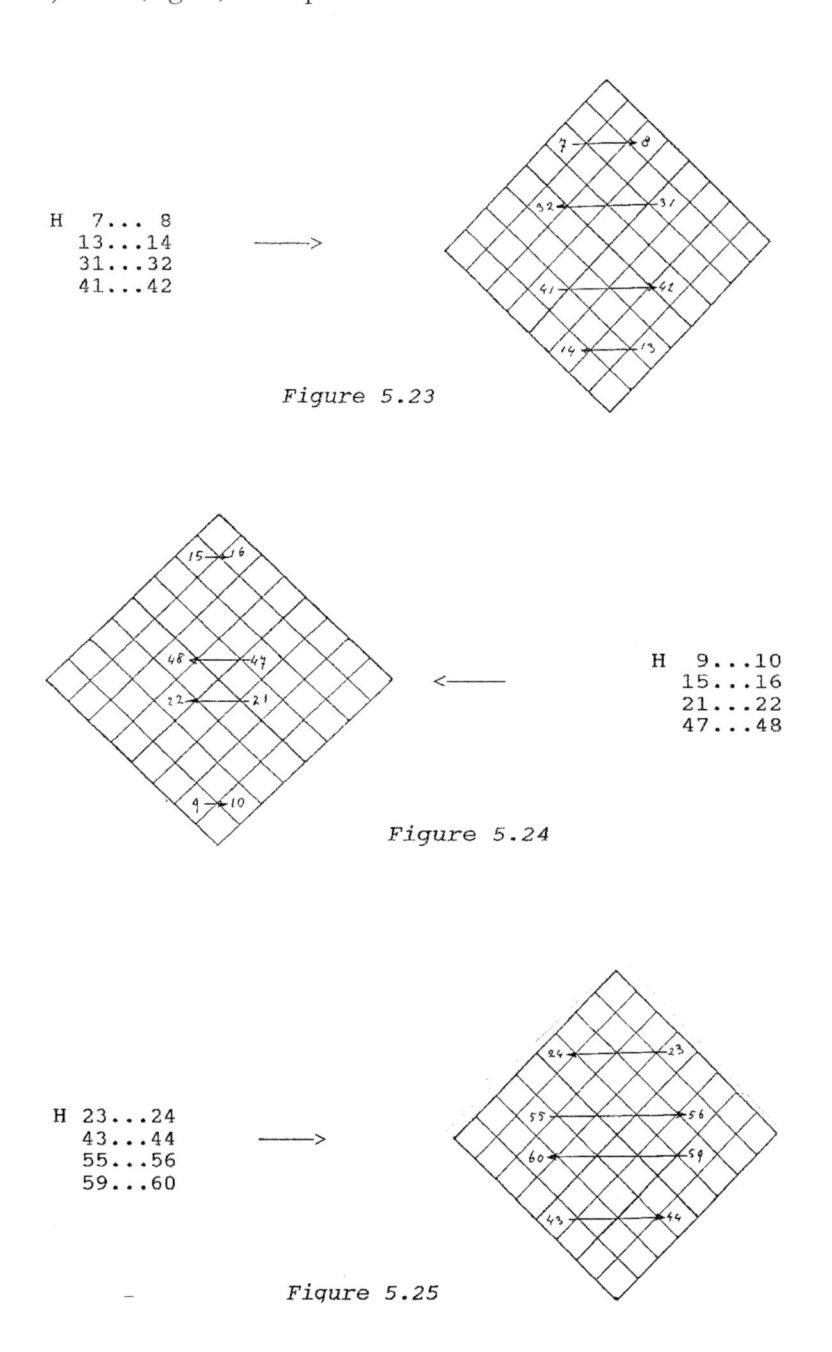

```
H  7... 8
   13...14        ——>
   31...32
   41...42
```

Figure 5.23

Figure 5.24

```
H  9...10
   15...16
   21...22
   47...48
```

```
H 23...24
  43...44         ——>
  55...56
  59...60
```

Figure 5.25

59

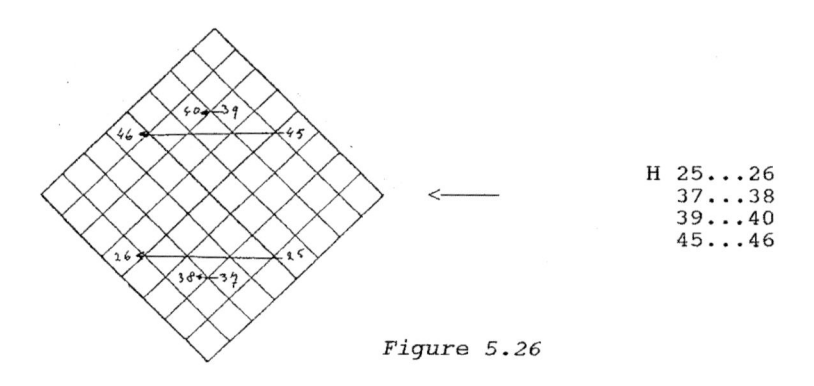

```
H  25...26
   37...38
   39...40
   45...46
```

Figure 5.26

```
H   1... 2
   27...28
   29...30
   61...62
```

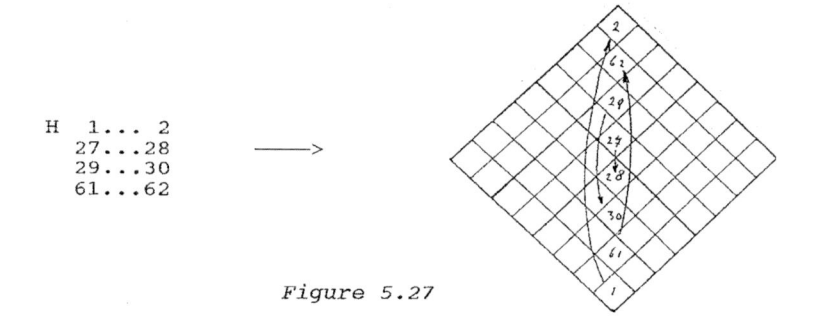

Figure 5.27

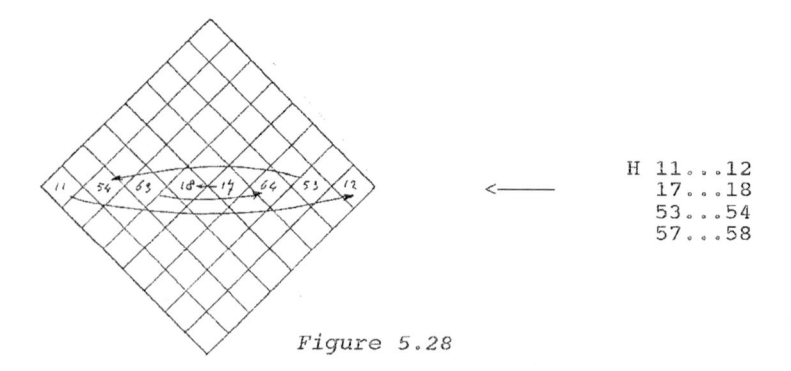

```
H  11...12
   17...18
   53...54
   57...58
```

Figure 5.28

```
H   3... 4
   19...20         ——>
   33...34
   49...50
```

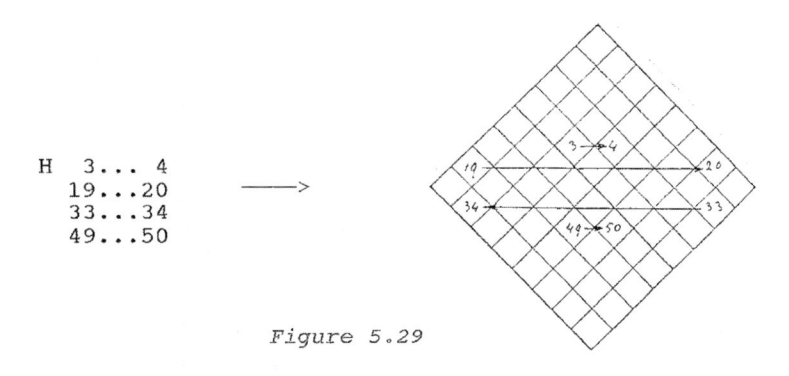

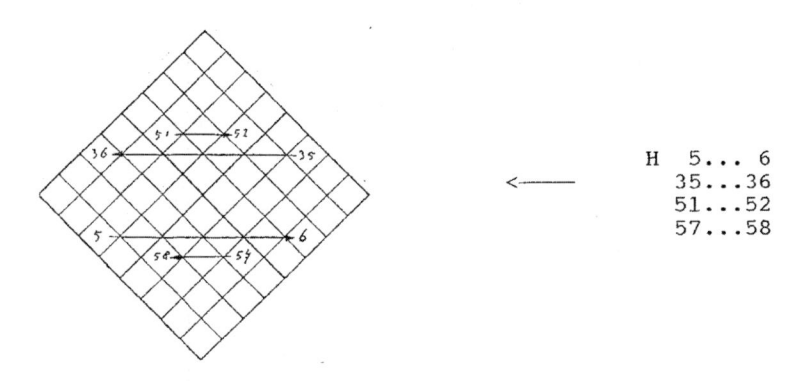

Figure 5.29

Figure 5.30

```
                        H   5... 6
            <——            35...36
                           51...52
                           57...58
```

We can also check pairs on their 'actual' difference, called 'co-index' by Terrence McKenna (The Invisible Landscape), to extract patterns out of a chosen square. When two Hexagrams are conjoined, its index is not identical with the movement marks. No co-index comes between the change of a Yang line to 'changing' Yang, since the co-index pertains to the Binary aspect of the Hexagrams. For example,:

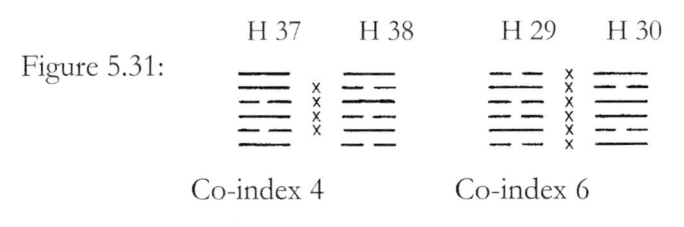

Figure 5.31:   H 37   H 38   H 29   H 30

           Co-index 4   Co-index 6

Below are the pairs we selected, with the co-indexes, "ci." beside them.

```
         ci.              ci.              ci.              ci.
 1 --  2 = 6    3 --  4 = 4    5 --  6 = 4   23 -- 24 = 2
27 -- 28 = 6   19 -- 20 = 4   35 -- 35 = 4   43 -- 44 = 2
29 -- 30 = 6   33 -- 34 = 4   51 -- 52 = 4   55 -- 56 = 2
61 -- 62 = 6   49 -- 50 = 4   57 -- 58 = 4   59 -- 60 = 2

         ci.              ci.              ci.              ci.
25 -- 26 = 4    7 --  8 = 2    9 -- 10 = 2   11 -- 12 = 6
37 -- 38 = 4   13 -- 14 = 2   15 -- 16 = 2   17 -- 18 = 6
39 -- 40 = 4   31 -- 32 = 2   21 -- 22 = 2   53 -- 54 = 6
45 -- 46 = 4   41 -- 42 = 2   47 -- 48 = 2   63 -- 64 = 6
```

If we now select a co-index and draw arrows in the square between the pairs to which they belong, we see a well-conceived symmetry of the textual numbering. Yet, again, the arrows lead to questions about whether certain pairs should be "switched". They are shown below (Fig. 5.32) in standard squares:

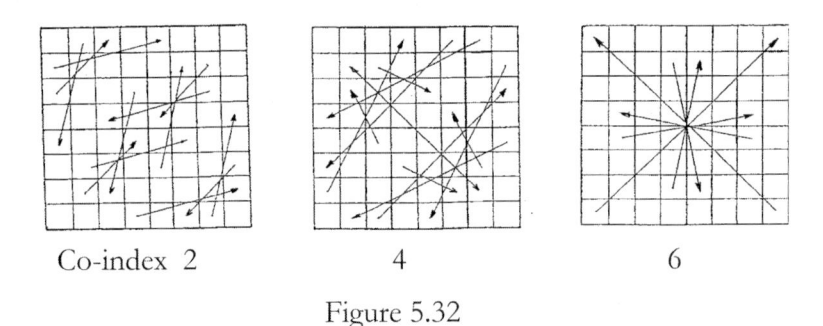

Co-index 2   4   6

Figure 5.32

Interested readers may frame other squares and check with arrows for more possible switches. The circle around the square provides the same chance. These examples separate odd and even pairs, leading to the same conclusions.

Figure 5. 33:

Figure 5.34:

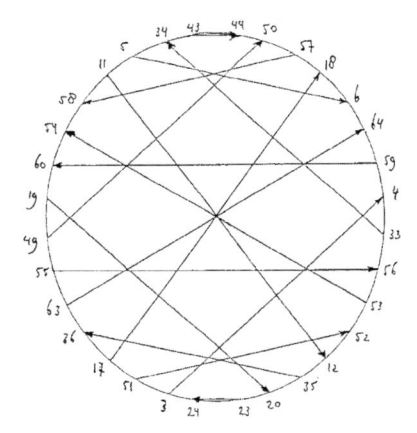

The I Ching conveys nature's continual balance and polarity in form and meaning; movement upward follows downward; Yang prevails then Yin, light/dark, active/passive, increase/decrease. In examining the 64 binary Hexagram image pairs in the order proscribed by the I Ching, we can see these universal principles.

Figure 5.35:

63

The lines of 24 pairs mirror each other by process of up-and-down inversion; 4 pairs of Yin/Yang conversion; 4 pairs do both. We will now examine those patterns and the energy flows they imply.

As we know, the universal Yin-Yang symbol (Fig. 5.36) shows the transformative nature of opposing and complimentary forces contained in a circle:

Figure 5.36

By reversing the two 'tears' so their points meet (Fig. 5.37), we see the figure-eight symbol of infinity emerge, appearing to be in motion:

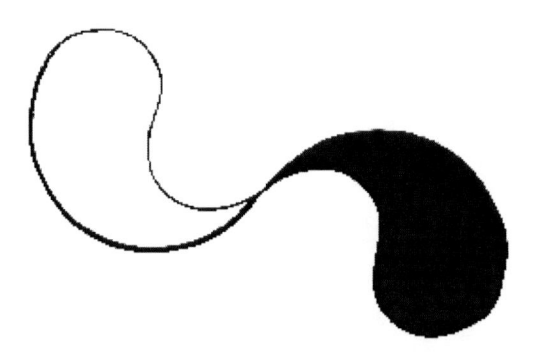

Figure 5.37

Like the Hexagrams pairs, energy flows seamlessly through this turning infinity symbol, back and forth as well as up and down. This beautiful depiction of infinity hidden within the classic circle of Yin and Yang reminds us that invisible forces circulate in endless rhythms in life, just as time – *and un-time* – spiral through and between experience. These concepts together will help us form another bridge of understanding between the wonderful structure inherent in the I Ching and its profound meaning.

A perfect symmetry of directional movement also exists between the I Ching square and surrounding circle of Hexagrams (Fig. 5.38).

For example:

Hexagram	Square	Circle
1	lower right corner	top (South)
2	upper left corner	bottom (North)
11	lower left corner	South-Easterly
12	upper right corner	North-Westerly
32, 57, 42, 51	the central 4 spaces	opposite pairs SW & NE

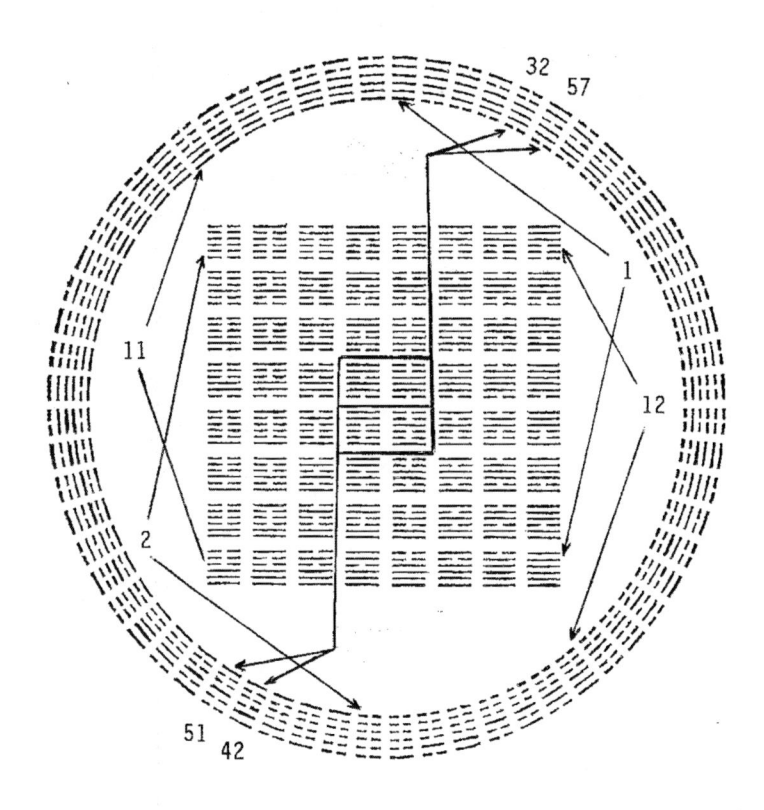

Figure 5.38

By connecting Hexagram pairs of up/down inversion with those that mirror them by Yin/Yang conversion, (Fig. 5.39, 5.40) the energy flow reveals the symbol of infinity!

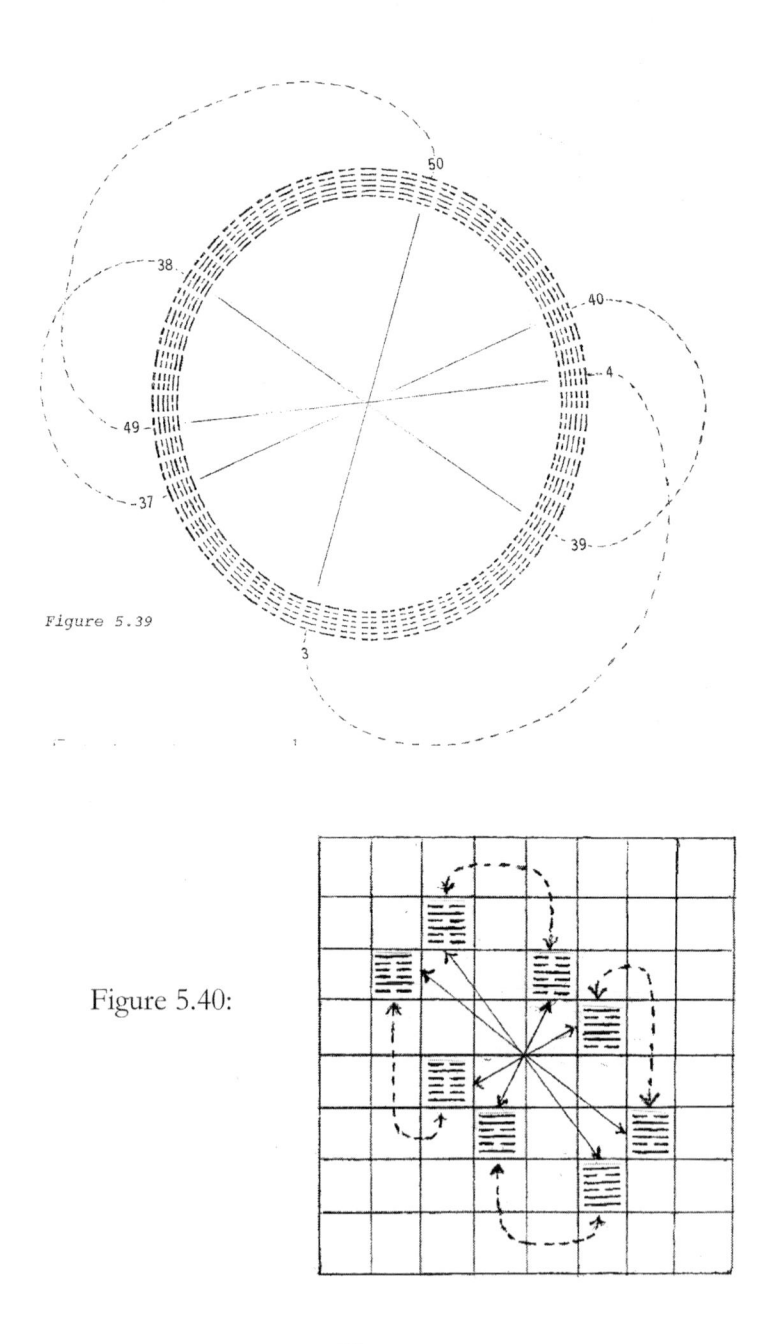

Figure 5.39

Figure 5.40:

This pattern (Fig. 5.41 and 5.42) in the square is the reverse of the previous example.

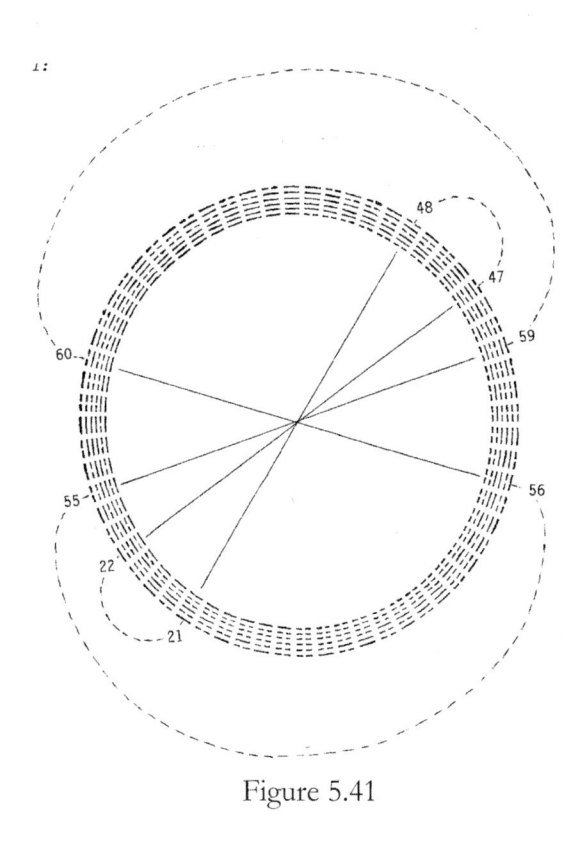

Figure 5.41

Figure 5.42:

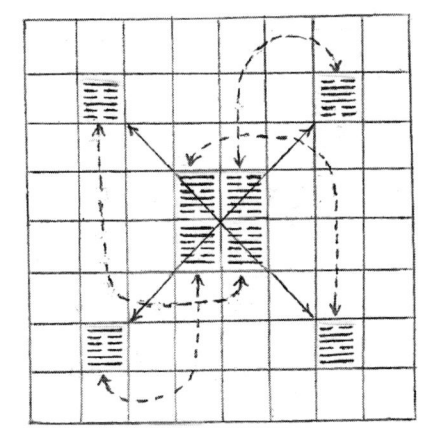

Here (Fig. 5.43 and 5.44) a different symmetry is in the square, with a butterfly-like pattern shown with the circle.

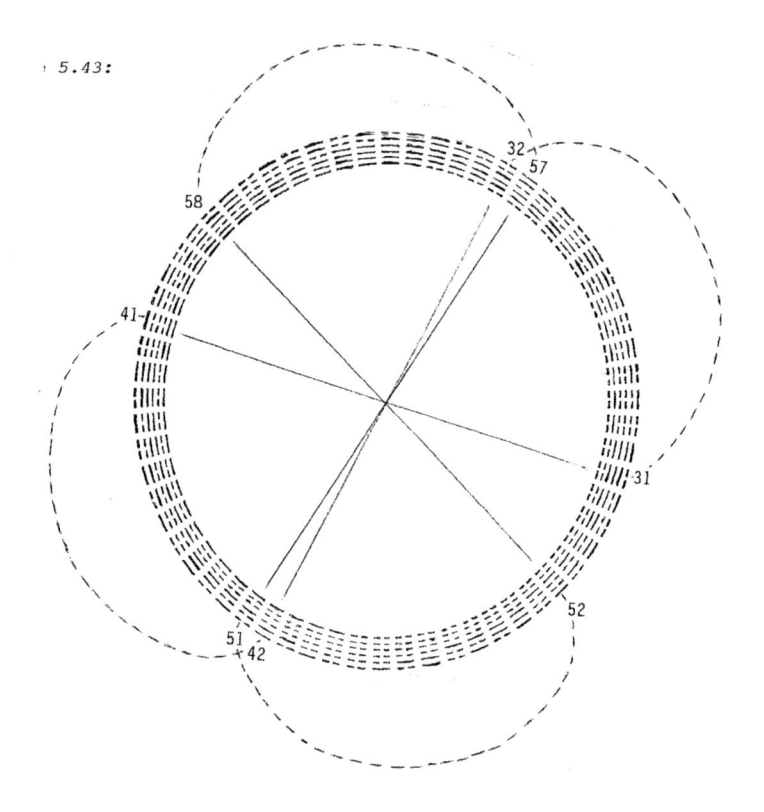

5.43:

Figure 5.44:

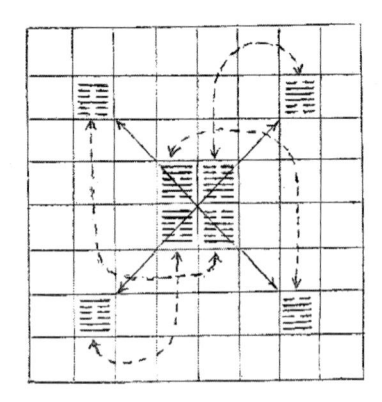

Energy flows through the circle (Fig. 5.45), as a lotus or rose. The same Hexagrams in the square's rim (Fig. 5.46) illustrates a similar energy pattern.

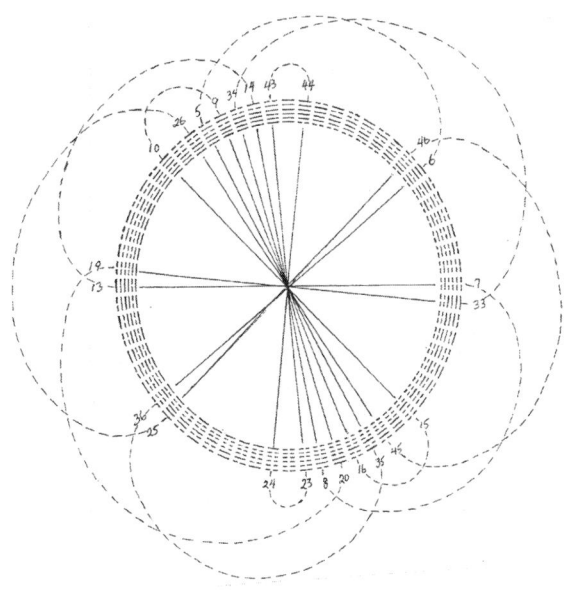

Figure 5.45

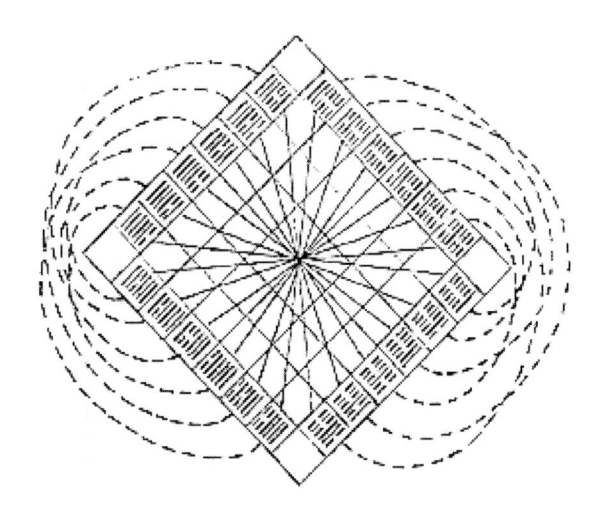

Figure 5.46

These Hexagrams' lines are internally arranged the same going up as well as down and are thus paired with their Yin/Yang opposites.

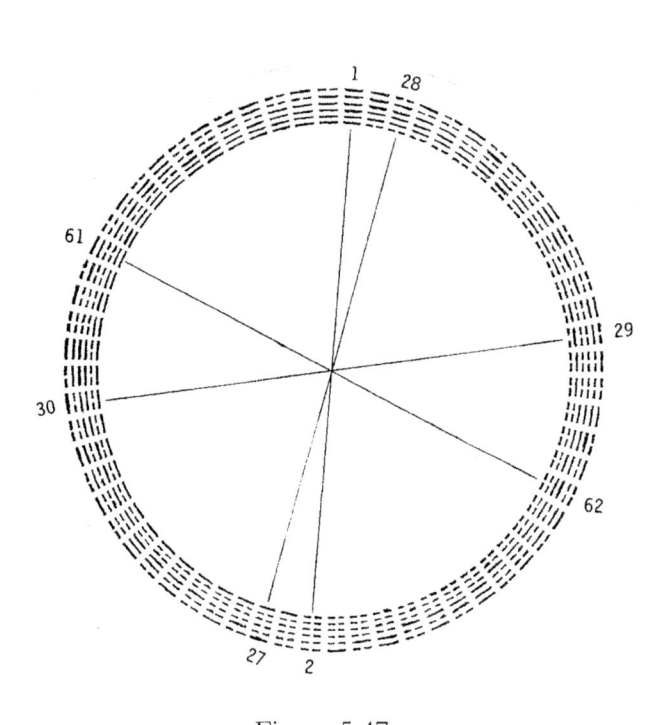

Figure 5.47

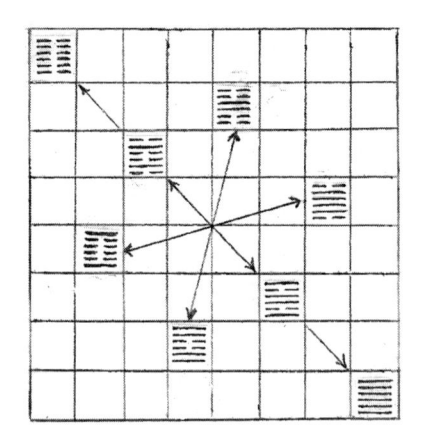

Figure 5.48

Each member of these pairs (Fig. 5.49 and 5.50) is both the up/down inversion and the Yin/Yang conversion of the other.

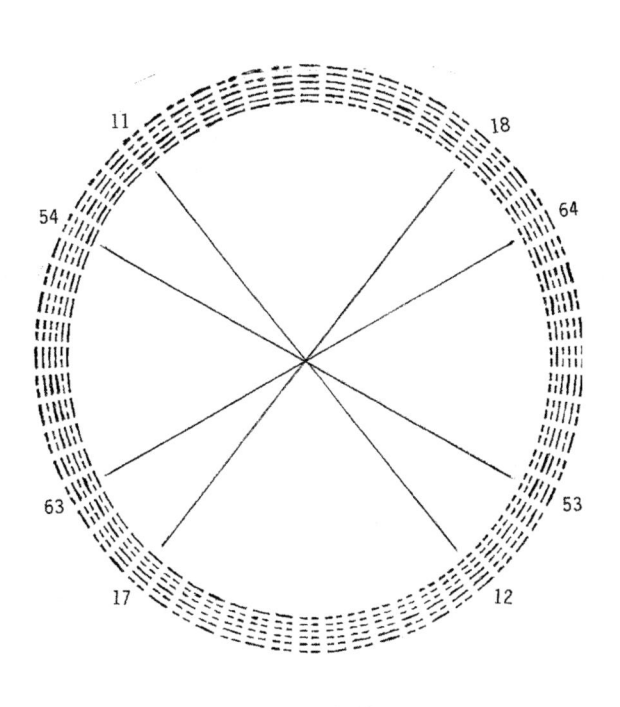

Figure 5.49

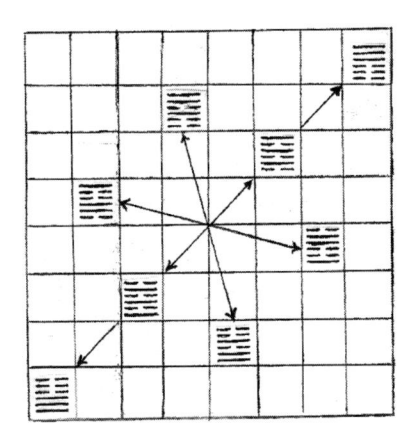

Figure 5.50

CHAPTER 6: DIVISIONS AND THE STAR

Hexagrams pairs are clearly an important aspect of the I Ching, which may explain why the textual sequence is arranged in opposite or inverted 'pairs.' As such, a co-index of 2, 4 or 6 is always between them. Checking the co-index between pairs, as suggested by Terrence McKenna, we note a curious fact; while 1 through 4 and 6 appear as co-index, no 5 appears.

Co-index:	1	2	3	4	6
	52 - 53	2 - 3	6 - 7	4 - 5	38 - 39
	60 - 61	12 - 13	18 - 19	8 - 9	
		16 - 17	20 - 21	10 - 11	
		22 - 23	24 - 25	14 - 15	
		26 - 27	30 - 31	34 - 35	
		28 - 29	40 - 41	50 - 51	
		36 - 37	44 - 45		
		42 - 43	46 - 47		
		54 - 55	56 - 57		
			58 - 59		
			62 - 63		
			64 - 1		

As this is not a balanced pattern, we can surmise that some pairs are turned or displaced. Pairs in the textual sequence are ordered on the principle of inversion; reading 'quantified moments' alternatively steps down and is coupled with an opposite Hexagram image. These opposite pairs all have a co-index of 6, with H 1 as their 'third' Triole member.

The little arrows below point to a possible numbering switch.

1 - 2	10 - 15	24 - 44	38 - 39
3 - 50 <-	11 - 12	25 - 46 <-	51 - 57
4 - 49	17 - 18	26 - 45	52 - 58
5 - 35	19 - 33	27 - 28	53 - 54
6 - 36	20 - 34	29 - 30	55 - 59
7 - 13	21 - 48 <-	31 - 41	56 - 60
8 - 14	22 - 47	32 - 42	61 - 62
9 - 19 <-	23 - 43	37 - 40 <-	63 - 64

Suspect, therefore, are the following numbers:

The 3 - 50   9 - 16   21 - 48   25 - 46   37 - 40
     4 - 49   10 - 15 22 - 47   26 - 45   38 - 39

Hexagram pairs, which, in the textual sequence, are opposite to one another, are a separate group that can be divided in two times four pairs (Fig. 6.1). We'll call them Group A and B.

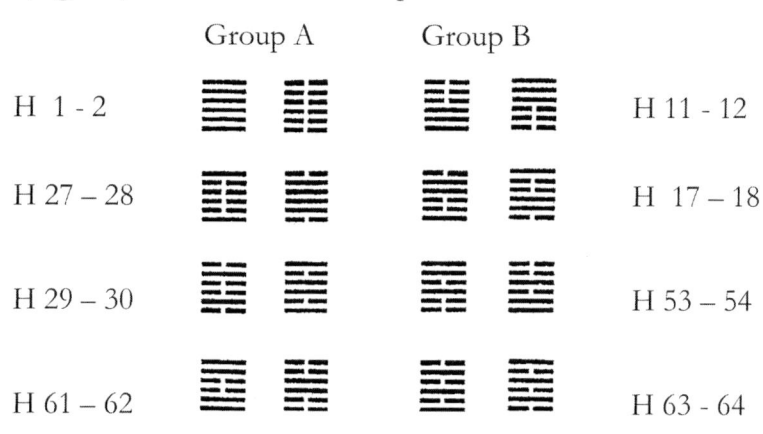

	Group A	Group B	
H 1 - 2			H 11 - 12
H 27 – 28			H 17 – 18
H 29 – 30			H 53 – 54
H 61 – 62			H 63 - 64

Figure 6. 1

The pairs are separated in two groups because while they all sort under Hexagram 1 and have co-index 6, Group A has an even number of Yang lines; Group B has three Yang lines. Moreover, the pairs in Group B are not only opposite, but are also inverted. This principle can be worked out for all other Hexagrams. For example (Fig. 6.2):

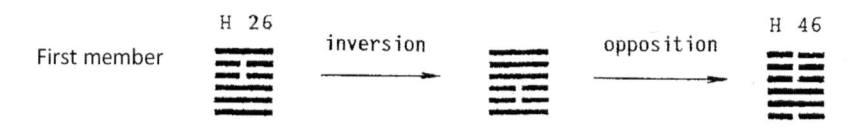

First member   H 26   inversion   →   opposition   →   H 46

Figure 6.2

Below, then, are the other pairs found that way:

```
3 - 49      19 - 34      31 - 42
4 - 50      20 - 33      32 - 41
5 - 36      21 - 47      37 - 39
6 - 35      22 - 48      38 - 40
7 - 14      23 - 44      51 - 58
8 - 13      24 - 43      52 - 57
9 - 15      25 - 45      55 - 60
10 - 16     26 - 46      56 - 59
```

While sorting these different kinds of pairs, we begin to see in what relation they stand to one another. Leaving out Group A and B for now, we now return to the pairs as arranged in the textual sequence. Sorting them again under the form of their binomial expression, the number of Yang lines (Fig. 6.3), we can make another division:

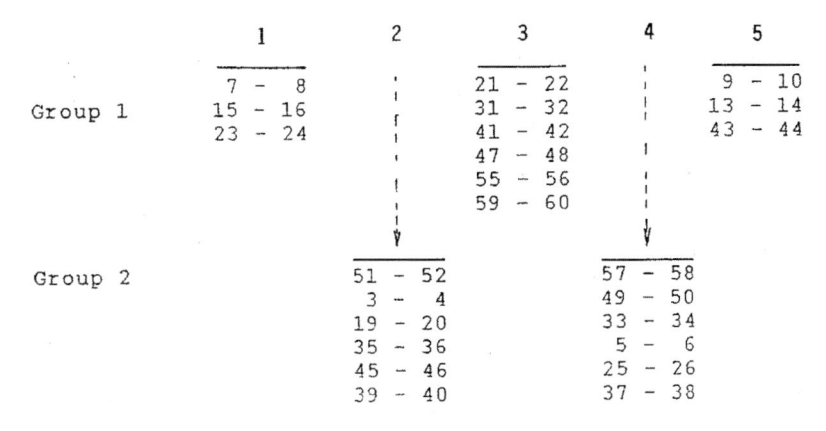

```
              1           2            3           4          5

           7  -  8                  21 - 22                 9 - 10
Group 1   15 - 16                  31 - 32                13 - 14
          23 - 24                  41 - 42                43 - 44
                                   47 - 48
                                   55 - 56
                                   59 - 60

Group 2               51 - 52                  57 - 58
                       3 -  4                  49 - 50
                      19 - 20                  33 - 34
                      35 - 36                   5 -  6
                      45 - 46                  25 - 26
                      39 - 40                  37 - 38
```

Figure 6.3

Combining the pairs into a 'block' form shows the relationship of the two kinds of pairs (Fig. 6.4), inverted and opposite, both in one pair:

H 7 — — — — → H 8

Inversion   - - - -
Opposing   . . . .
Inv. + Opp. _____

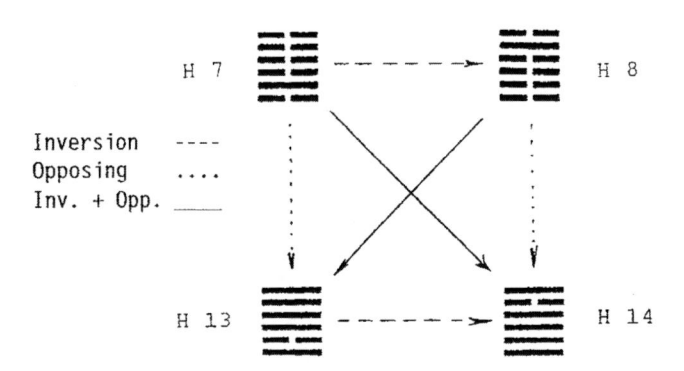

H 13 — — — — → H 14

Figure 6.4:

Diagonal pairs (crosswise) have both qualities; inverted and opposite. In sorting these pairs, we can assess the textual order, and confirm whether or not some of the numbers are displaced.

Completing Trioles from the pairs (Fig. 6.5), we can sort them as follows:

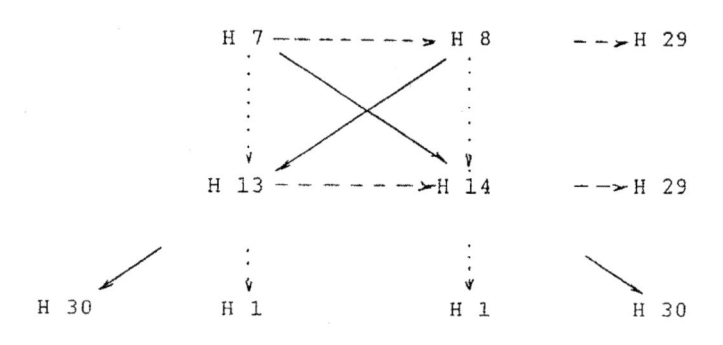

```
         H 7 -------> H 8            --> H 29
              \   /
               \ /
                X
               / \
              /   \
         H 13 -------> H 14           --> H 29

   ↙           ↓             ↓              ↘
 H 30        H 1           H 1            H 30
```

Figure 6.5

Combining now the other pairs of Group 1:

Hexagrams with one or five Yang lines (Fig. 6.6):

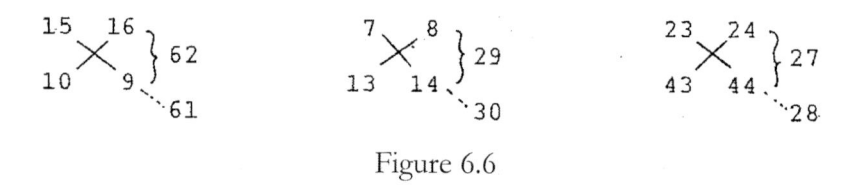

```
  15  16 ⎫              7   8  ⎫              23  24 ⎫
    X    ⎬ 62             X    ⎬ 29             X    ⎬ 27
  10   9 ⎭              13  14 ⎭              43  44 ⎭
         ⋱ 61                  ⋱ 30                  ⋱ 28
```

Figure 6.6

Hexagrams with three Yang lines (Fig. 6.7):

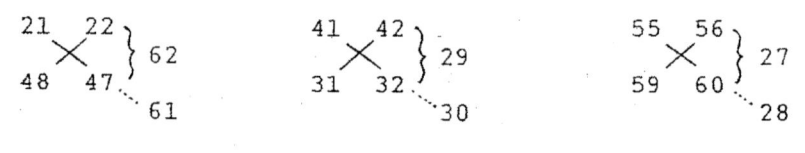

```
  21  22 ⎫              41  42 ⎫              55  56 ⎫
    X    ⎬ 62             X    ⎬ 29             X    ⎬ 27
  48  47 ⎭              31  32 ⎭              59  60 ⎭
         ⋱ 61                  ⋱ 30                  ⋱ 28
```

Figure 6.7

The horizontal divisions below are marked 'D', meaning 'Division sorted under' the Hexagram number that follows 'D':

    D 27:   23, 24, 43, 44, 55, 56, 59, 60
    D 29:   7, 8, 13, 14, 31, 32, 41, 42
    D 62:   9, 10, 15, 16, 21, 22, 47, 48

Doing the same operation with Group 2 (Fig. 6.8):

$$\begin{matrix} 25 & 26 \\ & \times \\ 46 & 45 \end{matrix} \Big\} 28 \\ \cdots 27$$

$$\begin{matrix} 51 & 52 \\ & \times \\ 57 & 58 \end{matrix} \Big\} 30 \\ \cdots 29$$

$$\begin{matrix} 3 & 4 \\ & \times \\ 50 & 49 \end{matrix} \Big\} 61 \\ \cdots 62$$

$$\begin{matrix} 37 & 38 \\ & \times \\ 40 & 39 \end{matrix} \Big\} 28 \\ \cdots 27$$

$$\begin{matrix} 5 & 6 \\ & \times \\ 35 & 36 \end{matrix} \Big\} 30 \\ \cdots 29$$

$$\begin{matrix} 19 & 20 \\ & \times \\ 33 & 34 \end{matrix} \Big\} 61 \\ \cdots 62$$

Figure 6.8

D 28: 25, 26, 37, 38, 39, 40, 45, 46
D 30:   5, 6, 35, 36, 51, 52, 57, 58
D 61:   3, 4, 19, 20, 33, 34, 49, 50

Working on the principle of the Hexagram's somewhat 'hidden' quality of being inverted and opposite in one image, first evident in Group B, we name the Group B equivalent with division D 1. The more obvious Group A, with its peculiar quality of 'non-invertability' or reading the same stepping up or down, is equivalent with division D 2. Sorting the 64 Hexagrams this way forms 8 divisions, each with eight Hexagrams with certain peculiarities. Division 1 is related to the Divisions 28, 30, and 61, due to the Hexagrams having an even number of Yang lines. Likewise, Division 2 is related to the Divisions 27, 29 and 62, due to the Hexagrams having an odd number of Yang lines.

```
              D 28         D 27
              D 30         D 29
    D 1 -------- D 61      D 62 -------- D 2
```

The Hexagrams of Group A thus form a Binomial curve:

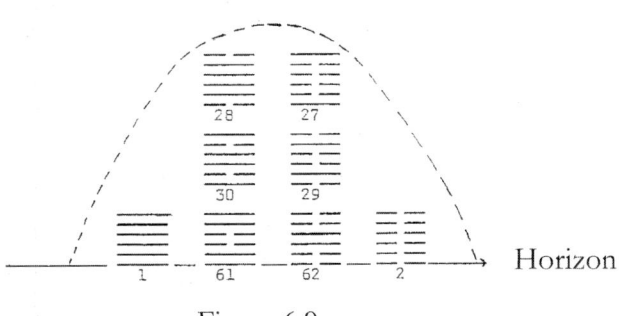

Figure 6.9

Looking at these Hexagrams of Group A, it is easy to see how they 'mirror' themselves; the upper trigram is reflected as a mirror image in the lower trigram (Fig. 6.10).

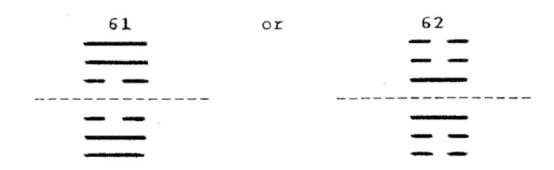

61 or 62

Figure 6.10

If we project D 1 and D 2 on a 'horizon' in accordance with a line from zero to one, or let's say from Yin to Yang (Fig. 6.11):

0 -------- 1

Figure 6.11

Then project the 8 divisions onto a circle (Fig. 6.12), D 1 and D 2 act as an axis or spoke turning the wheel, a beautiful image of change:

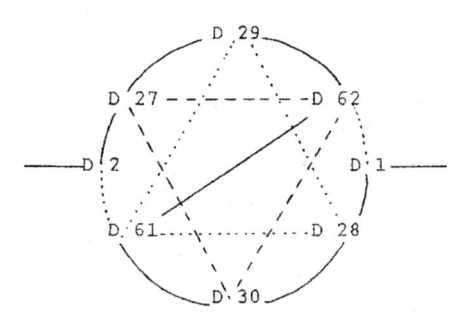

D 29
D 27 — D 62
D 2   D 1
D 61   D 28
D 30

Figure 6.12

We see that the divisions follow a closed circuit with the same series of Trigrams as in Fig. 5.8 and 5.9. To see its importance, we will arrange the Hexagrams' upper half 'mirror' images in that order, which shows trigrams Sun and Chen switched in this pattern (Fig. 6.13). This is the opposite of the usual trigram circle reputedly given by the sage Fu Hsi.

THE GIFT OF THE TORTOISE: NEW INSIGHTS INTO THE I CHING

Classic   Alternative

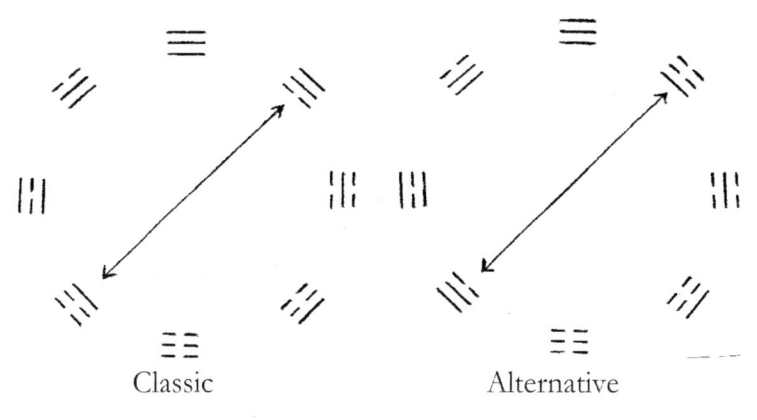

Figure 6.13

Starting at the top in the 'new' order (Fig. 6.14) with trigram **Chien**, going **counterclockwise** through trigram **Tui** and **Li**, we come to **Sun** instead of Chen, these three being named the daughters. We go then across to trigram **Chen**, next to **K'an** and **Ken**, ending with **K'un**.

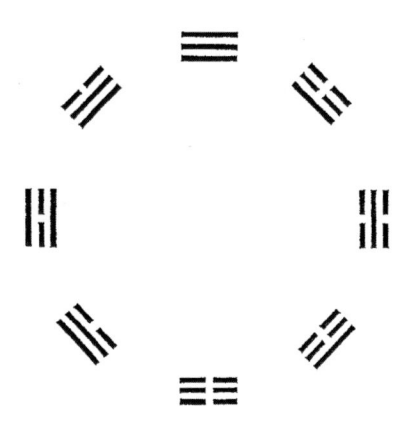

Chien → Tui → Li → Sun → Chen → K'an → Ken → K'un

Figure 6.14

Note how this order, used alongside the alternative square pattern of Figure 5.20, gives a different insight on the numbers' order, as shown in the following illustration (Fig. 615).

Figure 6.15

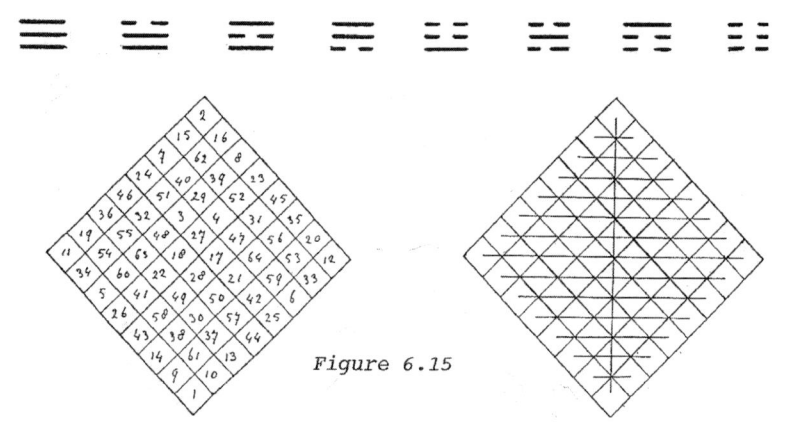

In old China, such an alternative placing of trigrams was used to ward off evil spirits. John Blofeld remarks, in an appendix to his magnificent book on the I Ching, that it may have been a misunderstanding due to the ignorance of popular fortune tellers, while staying open to the possibility of an internal reason that was not apparent to him. At first it looks like a different circle of Trigrams but it only appears so. You can view these Trigrams from inside out or from the outside inward. They are essentially the same sequence, and so are used alongside the alternative square; to the left, one way, to the right, the other way. If we fix Heaven and Earth at the ends, we see only six squares have this inner pattern, suggesting a rise of consciousness, through the 'planes.'

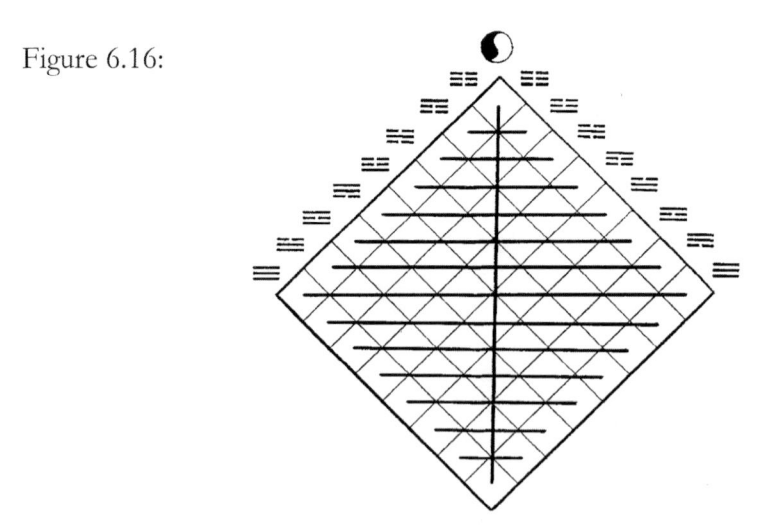

Figure 6.16:

Let's return to the Divisions, shown (Fig. 6.17) in a horizontal table:

```
D  2:    1 -  2    27 - 28    29 - 30    61 - 62
D 61:    3 -  4    19 - 20    33 - 34    49 - 50
D 30:    5 -  6    35 - 36    51 - 52    57 - 58
D 28:   25 - 26    37 - 38    39 - 40    45 - 46
D 27:   23 - 24    43 - 44    55 - 56    59 - 60
D 29:    7 -  8    13 - 14    31 - 32    41 - 42
D 62:    9 - 10    15 - 16    21 - 22    47 - 48
D  1:   11 - 12    17 - 18    53 - 54    63 - 64
```

Figure 6.17

While there is a certain order, all is not yet well. Let's now 'stretch' this table (Fig. 6.18), following the Traditional numbering order. Studying the numbers and placements, we must conclude that it is more chaotic than orderly, as the table is organized by the images of 'lines', or Binary appearance, not the given numbers.

D 2	1 - 2		27 - 28	29 - 30			61 - 62
D 61	3 - 4		19 - 20	33 - 34		49 - 50	
D 30	5 - 6			35 - 36		51 - 52	57 - 58
D 28			25 - 26	37 - 38	39 - 40	45 - 46	
D 27			23 - 24		43 - 44	55 - 56	59 - 60
D 29	7 - 8	13 - 14		31 - 32	41 - 42		
D 62	9 - 10	15 - 16	21 - 22			47 - 48	
D 1	11 - 12	17 - 18				53 - 54	63 - 64

Figure 6.18

Here is the argument: Making Trioles from pairs is still a Binary operation as it works on the law of odd and even. When you follow the flow through the circle (Fig. 6.19), you no longer need to use 'marks' since given two Hexagrams, you can always arrive at the third.

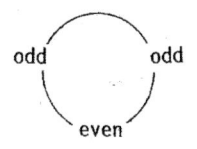

Figure 6.19

Knowing you can project the three Hexagrams onto the circle and consider them a 'whole', we shall name the first Hexagram 'Head', the second 'Shell' and the third 'Tail' to symbolize their function within the 'whole' (Fig. 6.20). This is similar to a basic family unite, where a husband is the family 'head', a wife protects and cares for the family, as a 'shell' and a child follows in the family's footsteps, like a 'tail'. Many other associates resonate with this pattern of three functions, such as the forces of affirmation, refutation and reconciliation, and the functions of beginning, middle and end.

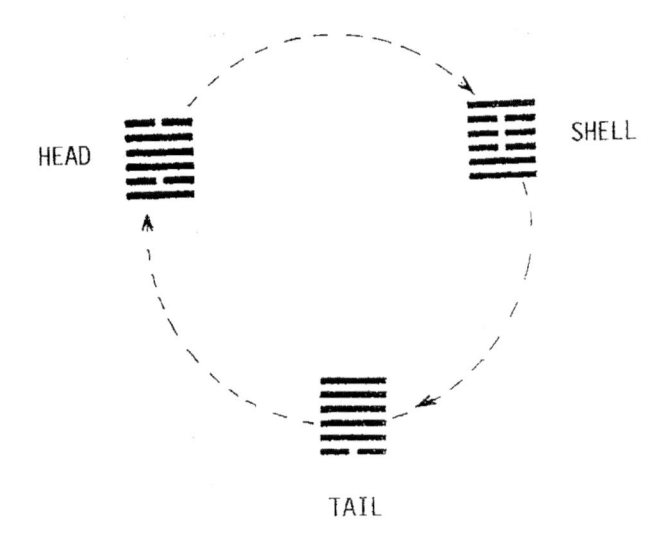

Figure 6.20

Sorting Hexagrams with Trioles gave the Divisions under the 'flag' of the 'Tail'. Each Division is a balanced whole, which we can see by separating them into trigrams (Fig. 6.21), using D 61 as our example:

Figure 6.21

The top and bottom rows each have a complete set of Trigrams, though it seems a few numbers might be better placed if they were attached to different Binary images. The relatedness of these Divisions is

THE GIFT OF THE TORTOISE: NEW INSIGHTS INTO THE I CHING

demonstrated by the fact that if, for instance, a D 27 Hexagram is associated with a D 62 Hexagram, a 'Tail' is derived from D 30. This holds true for the other Divisions. To see this clearly, we turn the D 1 / D 2 axis toward the front, so they both arrive in the center (Fig. 6.22), then follow the flow of Trioles.

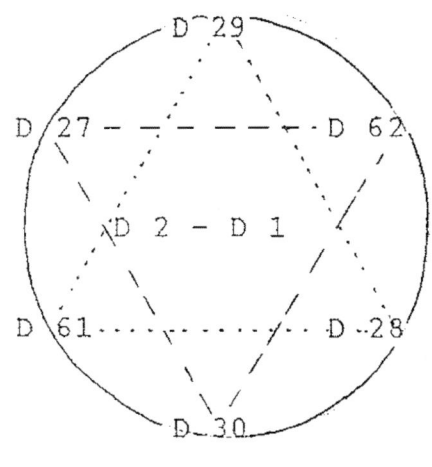

Figure 6.22

Putting the Hexagram images there (Fig. 6.23), we can deduce seven Trioles, while six more are a little 'invisible':

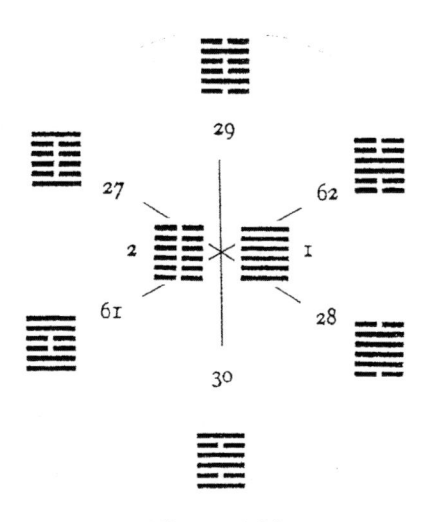

Figure 6.23

83

Therefore, a Triole 'communication' between Division members exists, a list of which follows:

Head or Shell in:	Tail in:	Head or Shell in:	Tail in:
D 1 D 61	D 62	D 1 D 1	D 2
D 1 D 62	D 61	D 1 D 2	D 1
D 61 D 62	D 1		
		D 2 D 27	D 27
D 1 D 29	D 30	D 27 D 27	D 2
D 1 D 30	D 29		
D 29 D 30	D 1	D 2 D 28	D 28
		D 28 D 28	D 2
D 1 D 27	D 28		
D 1 D 28	D 27	D 2 D 29	D 29
D 27 D 28	D 1	D 29 D 29	D 2
D 27 D 62	D 30	D 2 D 30	D 30
D 27 D 30	D 62	D 30 D 30	D 2
D 30 D 62	D 27		
		D 2 D 61	D 61
D 28 D 61	D 30	D 61 D 61	D 2
D 28 D 30	D 61		
D 30 D 61	D 28	D 2 D 62	D 62
		D 62 D 62	D 2
D 27 D 61	D 29		
D 27 D 29	D 61	D 2 D 2	D 2
D 29 D 61	D 27		
D 28 D 29	D 62		
D 28 D 62	D 29		
D 29 D 62	D 28		

Thus, the star pattern (Fig. 6.24) first appearing in our standard square and reputed to be 'classic' is fundamental to our discussion of Trioles.

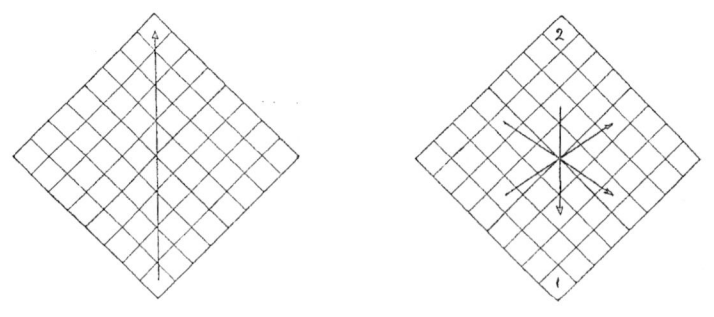

Figure 6.24

We can turn the axis of Hexagrams 1 and 2 to the front and center or lay it on the horizontal line (Fig. 6.25). The star, as an ancient symbol for Heaven, seems appropriate.

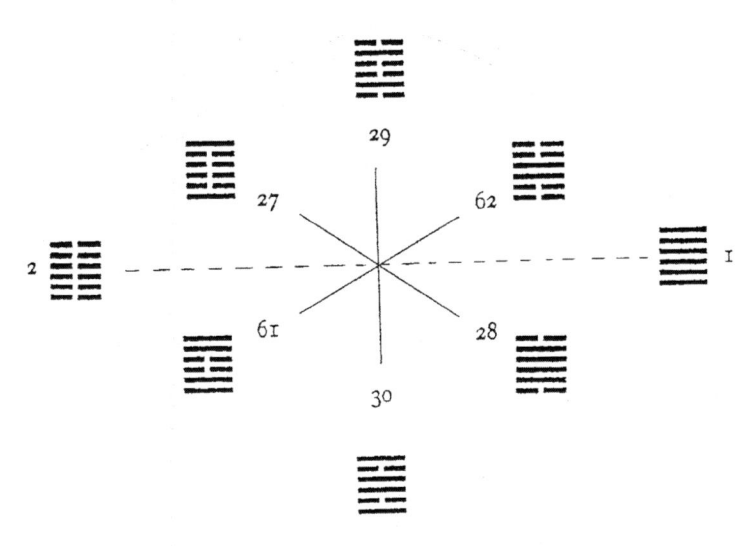

Figure 6.25

So, quite naturally, we place our Triole – our example oracle – on the star (Fig. 6.26), with the triangle pointing downward to symbolize the 'dramatic' processes on Earth.

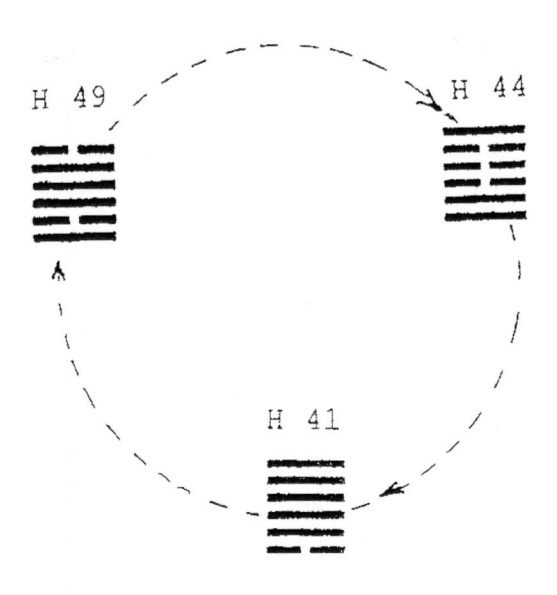

Figure 6.26

An invisible triangle points up, pertaining to a 'power' structure and concepts related to Heaven. We name the points of the star (Fig. 6.27), to assist us in evaluating the Hexagrams that appear at those points.

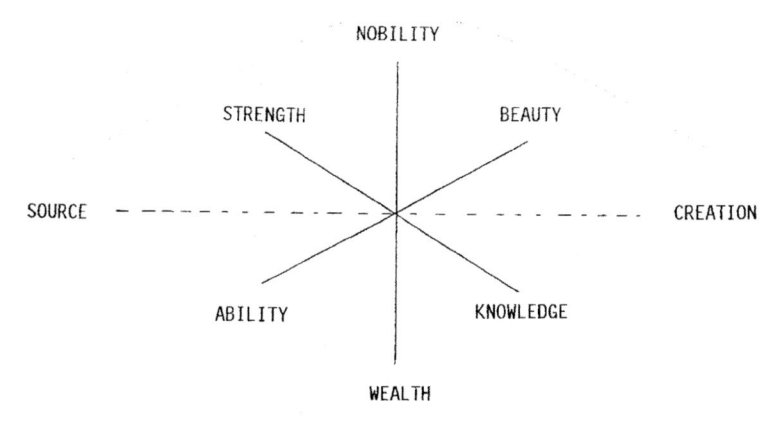

```
                    NOBILITY
                       |
         STRENGTH      |      BEAUTY
                  \    |    /
                   \   |   /
SOURCE  — — — — — — —  *  — — — — — — —  CREATION
                   /   |   \
                  /    |    \
         ABILITY       |      KNOWLEDGE
                       |
                    WEALTH
```

Figure 6.27

Although we think our names for the three Trioles positions fit 'par excellence,' they are somewhat arbitrary and may be otherwise named according to one's understanding of the basic direction, as with the names we have assigned to the axis points.

CHAPTER 7: REVERSE AND INTERIM HEXAGRAMS

Every Triole has, in its 'whole' set, five related Trioles with the same numbering. In our example, Triole 49...44...41, the six Trioles are:

```
H 49...44...41    H 44...41...49    H 41...49...44
H 41...44...49    H 49...41...44    H 44...49...41
```

As the I Ching was consulted as an oracle, we view the second line of Trioles as a 'reversed' set of the first line. Trioles generally are neither forward nor reversed; only when the oracle places them on the triangle, do we speak of a forward or reverse order in a 'Psychological Time' sequence. As we normally follow a clockwise direction for the odd and even flow, we will call it 'forward'. The opposite flow, for a reverse order of Hexagrams, related to the original Triole, can be studied to further understand a situation. By adding marks in a reverse flow, we see how marks in a reversed set of Hexagrams fall differently (Fig. 7.1).

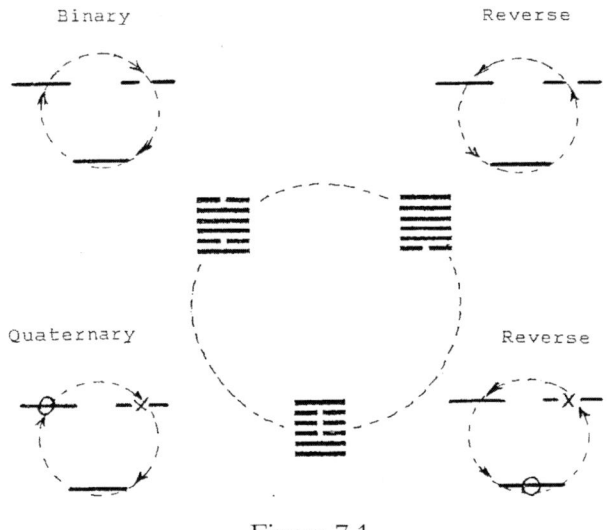

Figure 7.1

The quaternary rule still applies, thus Yang becomes changing Yang, which in turn becomes changing Yin. You can easily find the Triole numbers of the Hexagrams in the reverse order by referring to explanations in Chapter Four. In this chapter, we will also show how, by splitting marked Hexagrams into marked Trigrams, we can form tables to look up the corresponding quaternary number values.

Once you understand the logic of the quaternary system and how to use it, as outlined in the previous chapters, you can use a shorter method to find the quaternary value of a marked Hexagram, or to find which marked Hexagram corresponds to any quaternary value, as you will see in the Tables provided.

The numerical value of any Hexagram is the sum of the upper and lower 'Tri-grams' half-values. Marked Hexagrams are a Base 4 counting system, so the 2nd and 3rd lines increase in increments of 4, up to 63, while the upper three lines increase in increments of 64, up to 4032. To determine the value of any Hexagram from 0 to 4096, add the upper and lower Tri-gram values. Each Yin (0), Yang (1), Changing Yin (2) and Changing Yang (3), is a multiple of the value of that line. Using H 49, Revolution (Fig. 7.2), as an example.

Figure 7.2:

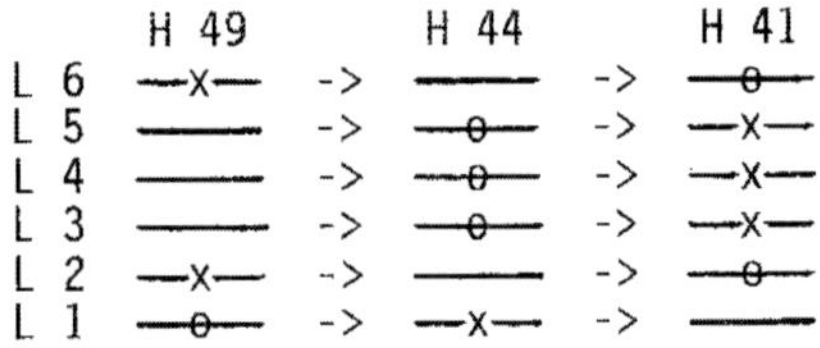

```
              H 49           H 44          H 41
       L 6   —x—    ->   ———     ->   —o—
       L 5   ———    ->   —o—     ->   —x—
       L 4   ———    ->   —o—     ->   —x—
       L 3   ———    ->   —o—     ->   —x—
       L 2   —x—    ->   ———     ->   —o—
       L 1   —o—    ->   —x—     ->   ———
```

Adding the upper and lower Tri-grams sums (Fig. 7.3) gives us 2395.

Figure 7.3:

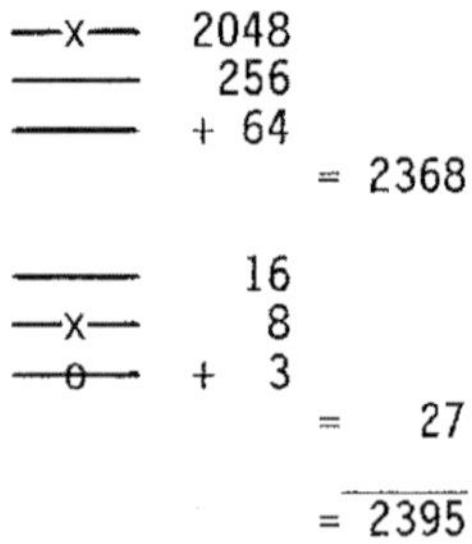

```
          —x—    2048
          ———     256
          ———   +  64
                      = 2368

          ———      16
          —x—       8
          —o—   +   3
                      =   27
                      ─────
                      = 2395
```

To derive the Triole, follow the odd/even rule to H 44, Meeting, then to H 41, Simple, which returns to H 49, Revolution, (Fig. 7.4).

THE GIFT OF THE TORTOISE: NEW INSIGHTS INTO THE I CHING

Figure 7.4:

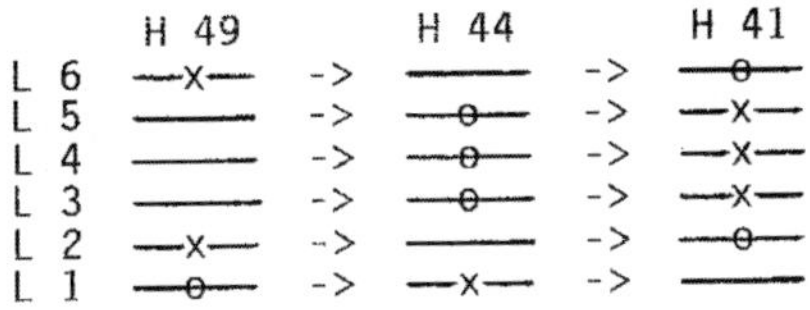

```
          H 49        H 44        H 41
L 6  --x--   ->  -----  ->  --o--
L 5  -----   ->  --o--  ->  --x--
L 4  -----   ->  --o--  ->  --x--
L 3  -----   ->  --o--  ->  --x--
L 2  --x--   ->  -----  ->  --o--
L 1  --o--   ->  --x--  ->  -----
```

Figure 7.5:   **Lower Tri-grams with Changes:**

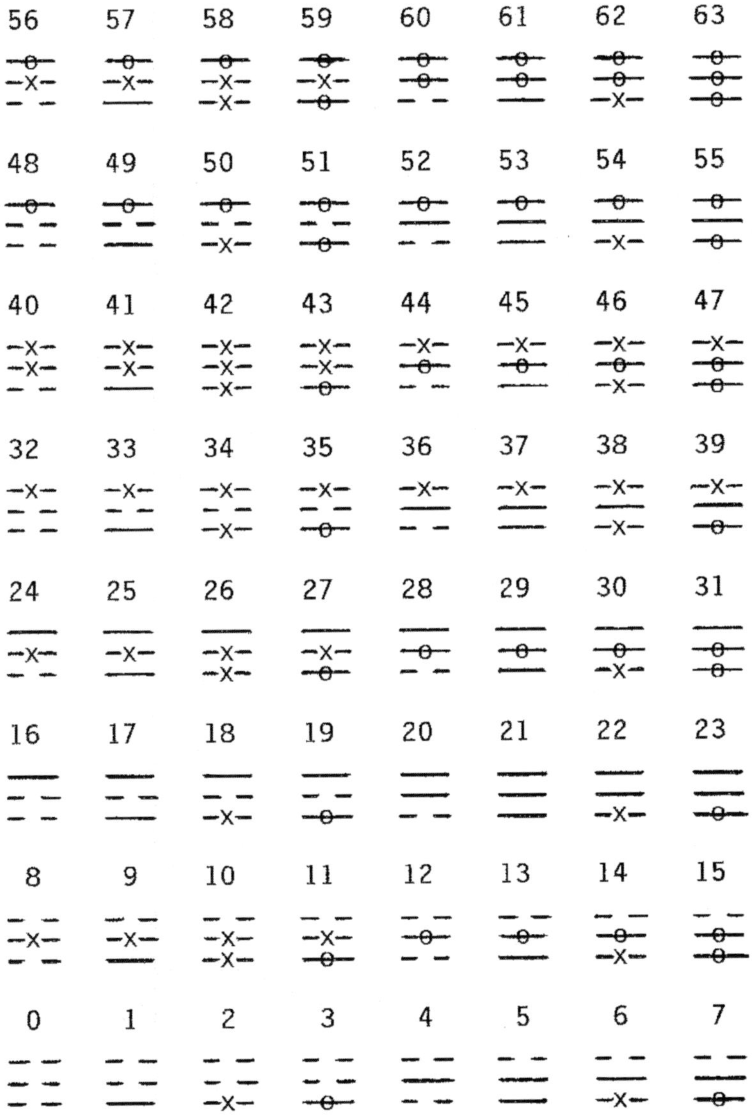

| 56 | 57 | 58 | 59 | 60 | 61 | 62 | 63 |

| 48 | 49 | 50 | 51 | 52 | 53 | 54 | 55 |

| 40 | 41 | 42 | 43 | 44 | 45 | 46 | 47 |

| 32 | 33 | 34 | 35 | 36 | 37 | 38 | 39 |

| 24 | 25 | 26 | 27 | 28 | 29 | 30 | 31 |

| 16 | 17 | 18 | 19 | 20 | 21 | 22 | 23 |

| 8 | 9 | 10 | 11 | 12 | 13 | 14 | 15 |

| 0 | 1 | 2 | 3 | 4 | 5 | 6 | 7 |

Figure 7.6: **Upper Tri-grams with Changes:**

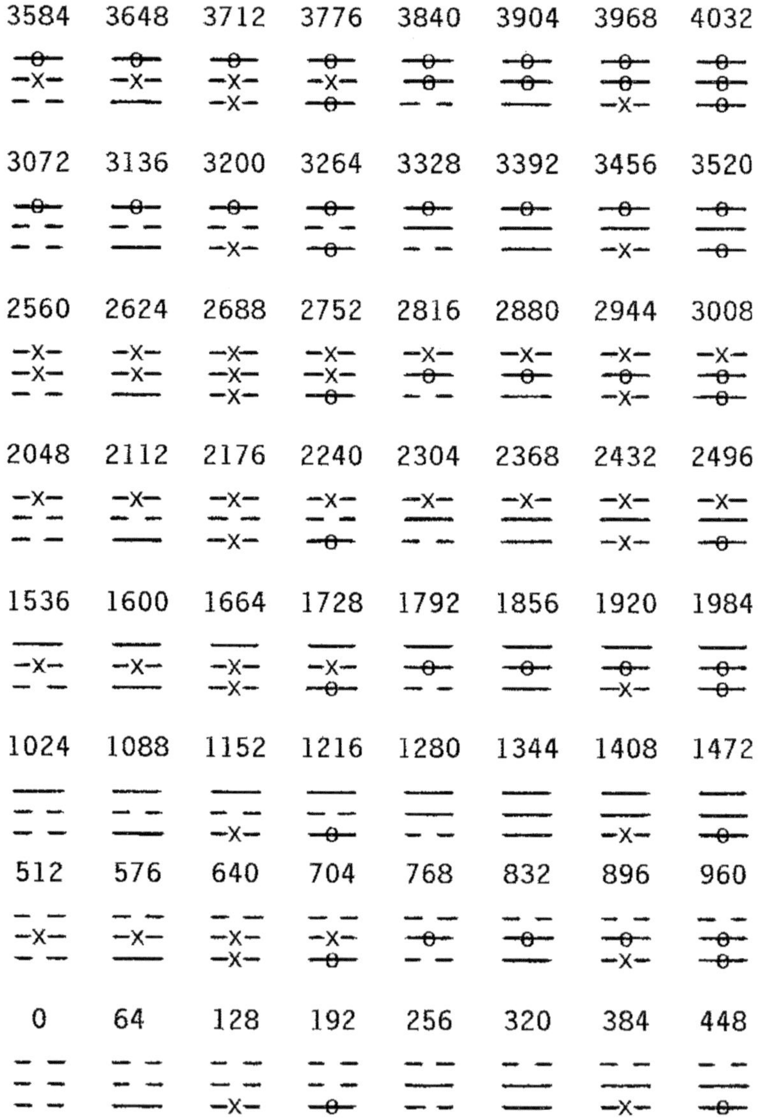

3584	3648	3712	3776	3840	3904	3968	4032
3072	3136	3200	3264	3328	3392	3456	3520
2560	2624	2688	2752	2816	2880	2944	3008
2048	2112	2176	2240	2304	2368	2432	2496
1536	1600	1664	1728	1792	1856	1920	1984
1024	1088	1152	1216	1280	1344	1408	1472
512	576	640	704	768	832	896	960
0	64	128	192	256	320	384	448

Our next illustration shows our original Triole 49…44…41 in its natural flow (Fig. 7.7), starting with **Revolution**, with marks that change it into **Meeting**, whose marks then leads us to **Simple**.

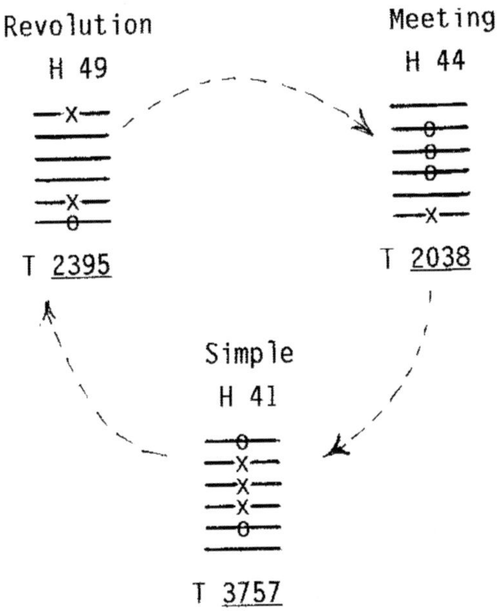
Revolution
H 49
T 2395
Meeting
H 44
T 2038
Simple
H 41
T 3757

Figure 7.7:

The Reverse Triole (Fig. 7.8) flows the opposite, with different marks:

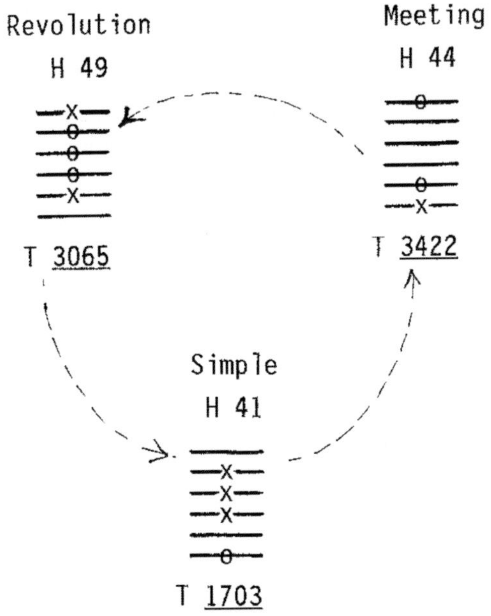
Revolution
H 49
T 3065
Meeting
H 44
T 3422
Simple
H 41
T 1703

Figure 7.8:

Placed side by side, an interesting pattern emerges:

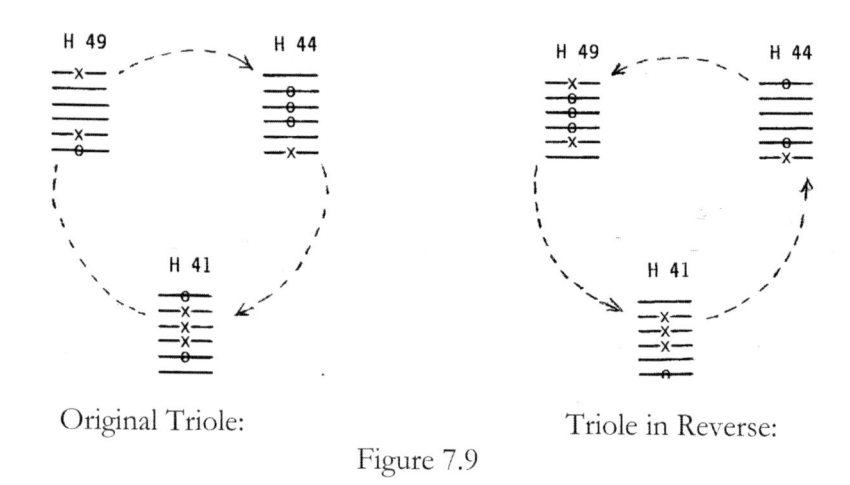

```
   H 49           H 44              H 49           H 44
  —x—            ———              —x—            ———
  ———            —o—              —o—            ———
  ———            —o—              —o—            ———
  —x—            —o—              —o—            —o—
  —o—            —x—              —x—            —x—

        H 41                              H 41
       —o—                                ———
       —x—                                —x—
       —x—                                —x—
       —x—                                —x—
       —o—                                —o—
       ———                                ———
```

Original Triole: Triole in Reverse:

Figure 7.9

The pattern is clear when we pair the Hexagrams together:

```
   Original      Reversed      The Pattern
    H 49           H 49           H 49
    —x—            —x—          X — — X
    ———            —o—          ——— O
    ———            —o—          ——— O
    ———            —o—          ——— O
    —x—            —x—          X — — X
    —o—            ———          O ———

    H 44           H 44           H 44
    ———            —o—          ——— O
    —o—            ———          O ———
    —o—            ———          O ———
    —o—            ———          O ———
    ———            —o—          ——— O
    —x—            —x—          X — — X

    H 41           H 41           H 41
    —o—            ———          O ———
    —x—            —x—          X — — X
    —x—            —x—          X — — X
    —x—            —x—          X — — X
    —o—            ———          O ———
    ———            —o—          ——— O
```

Figure 7.10

THE GIFT OF THE TORTOISE: NEW INSIGHTS INTO THE I CHING

Yang lines appear in an opposing order; Yin lines are the same in both directions, which would still be true if they were unmarked. Reverse Hexagrams *'look back' in time,* suggesting the quality of a **shadow** following us. By **shading** each Reversed Hexagram 'o' (Fig. 7.11), we sharpen the marks' contrast.

Hexagram 49:

Hexagram 44:

Hexagram 41:

Figure 7.11

A shorthand method to state the *Original-and-Reversed* Trioles uses only the Yin and Yang marks (Fig. 7.12). By eliminating the lines and one 'x', since it repeats, the result is a simple column of six marks, shown below, to the right.

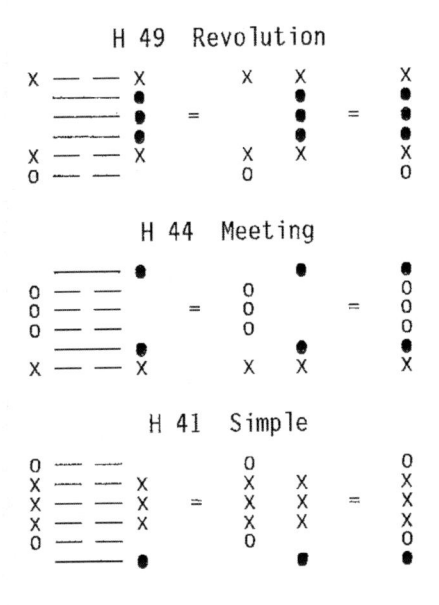

H 49   Revolution

H 44   Meeting

H 41   Simple

Figure 7.12:

With an unmarked Yin line, we would write '—' in place of 'x'.
Our Original Triole (Fig. 7.13), and it's Reverse (Fig. 7.14), are below.

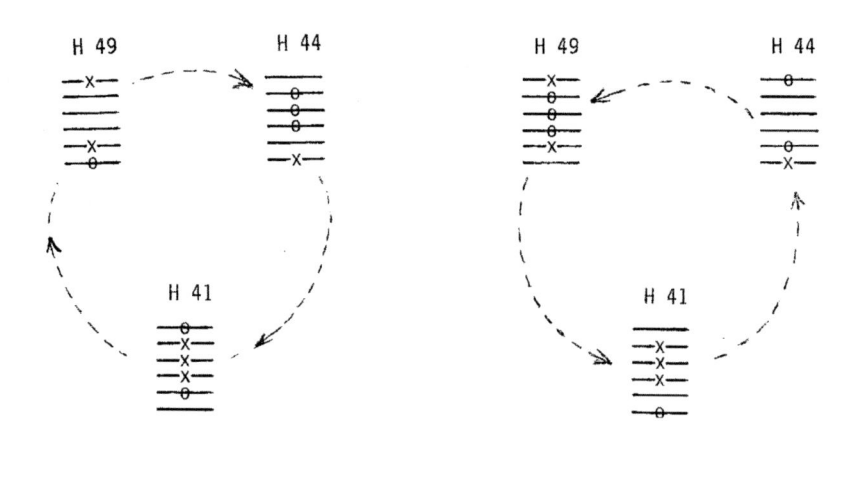

Figure 7.13   Figure 7.14:

We can combine them into 3 marked columns, shown in sequence below, with our spiraling Psychological Time-line (Fig. 7.15), and then using x and o for the future-oriented line to read, and x and shaded-o for the past-oriented line of text to read (Fig. 7.16):

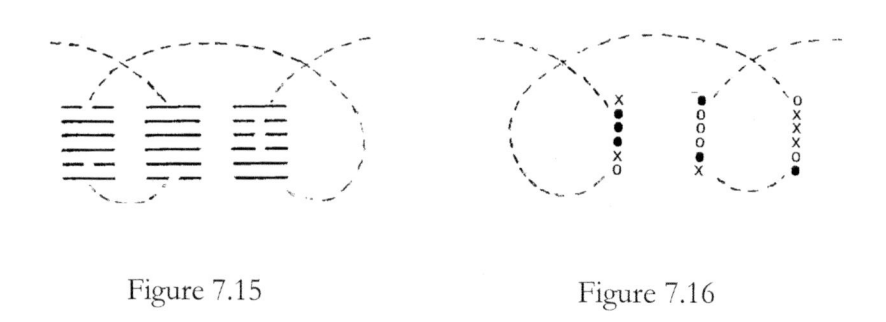

Figure 7.15   Figure 7.16

We call the 6-pointed star, on which we have set much importance, a 'Logon.' If we now turn the axis of H 1 and H 2, so that Hexagram 2 occupies the center, we gaze, symbolically, toward the star-source and, thus back in time (Fig. 7.17).

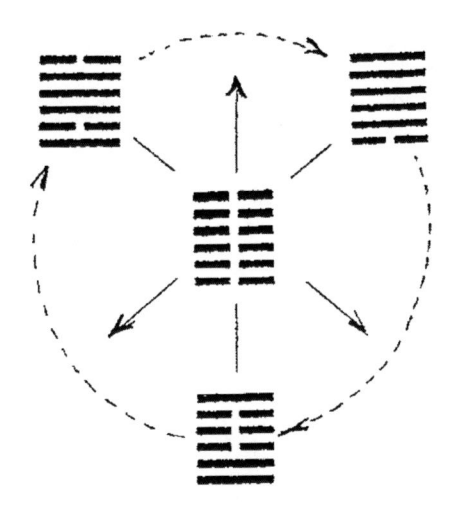

Figure 7.17

Making the Trioles crosswise (Fig. 7.18), the reverse set appears. In this way, we see that it is justified to view them with the original Triole.

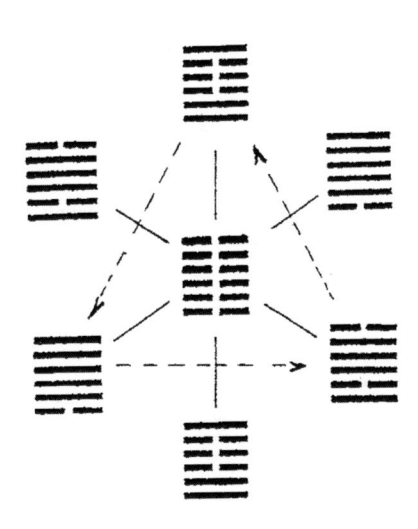

Figure 7.18

Setting the reverse Triole on the Logon gives it an additional meaning.

Interim Hexagrams

Since each Triole Hexagram becomes the next, we can explore the numerical relationship between their quaternary values (Fig. 7.19).

Revolution	Meeting	Simple
H 49	H 44	H 1
T 2395	T 2038	T 3757

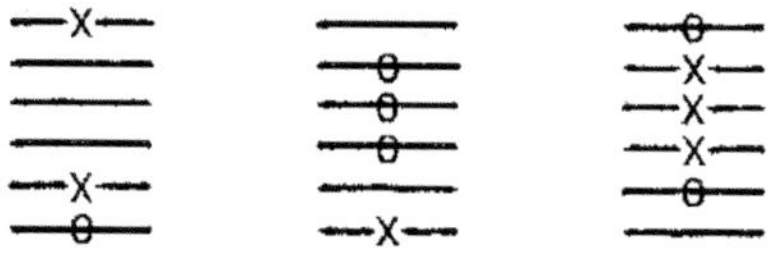

Figure 7.19

We find their numerical differences by subtracting one from the other; T 2395 minus T 2038, T 3757 minus T 2038 and T 3757 minus T 2395:

```
(H 49)   T 2395      (H 41)   T 3757      (H 41)   T 3757
(H 44) - T 2038      (H 44) - T 2038      (H 49) - T 2395
       =   357             = 1719               = 1362
```

The answers contain a perfect internal relationship:

```
   357              1719              1719
+ 1362       or  -  357       or   - 1362
  ----              ----               ----
= 1719            = 1362             =  357
```

These three values describe the numerical difference between Triole Hexagrams, measuring, as it were, the Psychological Time between them, similar to how Un-time jumps imperceivably between moments. We can translate these values (Fig. 7.20) into 'Interim Hexagrams'.

T 357	T 1719	T 1362
Joyous Lake	The Great Nourisher	Retreat

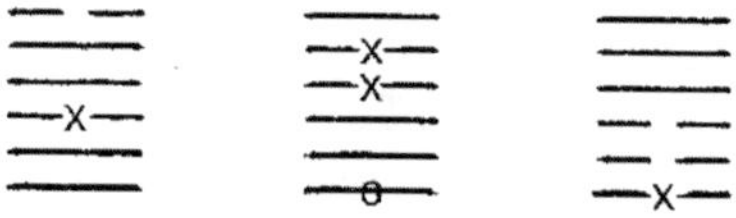

Figure 7.20

THE GIFT OF THE TORTOISE: NEW INSIGHTS INTO THE I CHING

Marked to reflect their Quaternary values, Interim Hexagrams form three new Trioles. Without marks, using the Odd/Even Rule, the basic Interim Hexagram images form one Binary Triole. To further extend this internal progression of Trioles is possible but would remove us too far from the original Triole and personal matter or concern in question.

Using our example, let's visualize the progression of the original Triole (Fig. 7.21): 49…44…41, shown below on the left in bold print, and the Interim Hexagrams between them, derived from their numerical differences, shown on the right:

H 49: Revolution   H 44: Meeting

T 2395   minus   T 2038   =   T 357

H 58: Joyous Lake

H 41: Simple   H 44: Meeting

T 3757   minus   T 2038   =   T 1719

H 26: Great Nourisher

H 41: Simple   H 49: Revolution

T 3757   minus   T 2395   =   T 1362

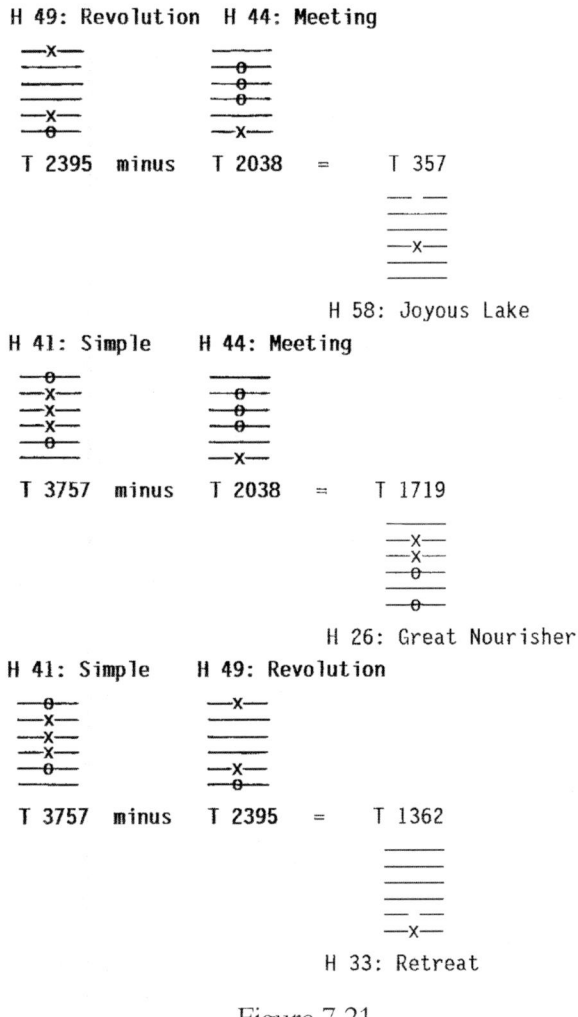

H 33: Retreat

Figure 7.21

Below, the relationship between these Hexagrams is shown with our perspective of Time and Un-Time with 3 connecting loops overlapping to form a curved triangle in the central space:

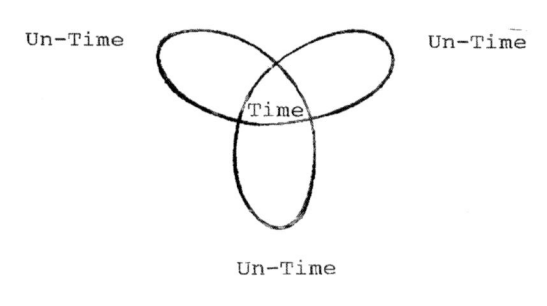

Figure 7.22

The original Triole is **in Time**; the 3 Interim Hexagrams in **Un-Time**:

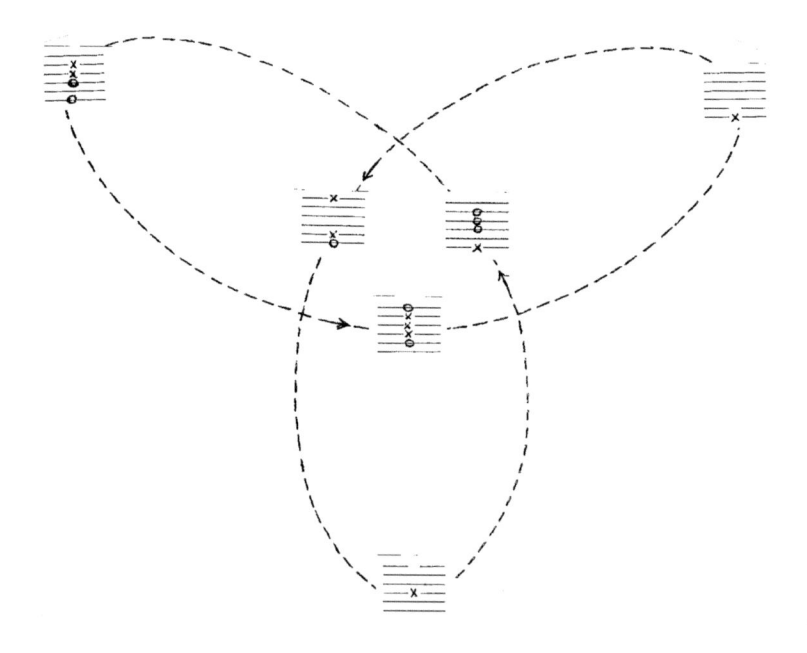

Figure 7.23

This demonstrates the abstract beauty and mathematical logic of the quaternary system and shows that the many possible changes of the I

Ching are, indeed as subtle in their nuances as life itself. Bearing in mind that Interim Hexagrams exist in the 'jump' of Un-time between perceivable moments, when interpreting them relative to the Oracle, their significance lies beyond the realm of our physical senses. They cannot, therefore, be proved nor disproved.

Herein, we are exploring **meta**physical realms, where contact and communication with out-of-body, sentient beings – or 'Invisibles' – is as commonplace to those who are receptive, as the notion of talking to a friend by phone is to most modern people. 'Interim Hexagrams' serve as a 'wire line' through which 'messages' can be transmitted.

To receive spiritual guidance from 'Invisibles', whose uplifting presence is never intrusive, we must 'invite' them into our lives. If we do, our consciousness gently rises to higher planes that transcend the dramas of earthly karma. Messages received as a result of Interim Hexagrams are to be considered as a gift from a benign source, without obligation.

Using our example, Triole 49…44…41, we will open the 'gift' using Richard Wilhelm's translation, The I Ching: Book of Changes, and our original verses in Questioning the Oracle: The I Ching for more insight.

Between H 49, Revolution and H 44, Meeting, is **H 58, Joyous Lake**, with one mark (Fig. 7.24). As before, the number of changes is the line to read, so the first line describes the spiritual climate surrounding the person who had anticipated a meeting.

Figure 7.24:

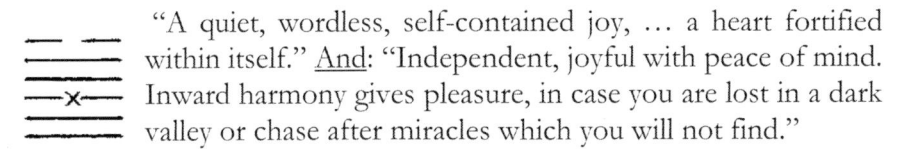

"A quiet, wordless, self-contained joy, … a heart fortified within itself." And: "Independent, joyful with peace of mind. Inward harmony gives pleasure, in case you are lost in a dark valley or chase after miracles which you will not find."

Between H 44 Meeting and H 41 Simple is **H 26 The Great Nourisher**, with 4 marks (Fig. 7.25), so line 4 describes the meeting's subtle effect on those involved.

Figure 7.25:

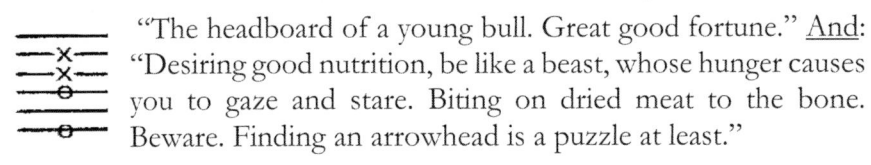

"The headboard of a young bull. Great good fortune." And: "Desiring good nutrition, be like a beast, whose hunger causes you to gaze and stare. Biting on dried meat to the bone. Beware. Finding an arrowhead is a puzzle at least."

Between H 41, Simple and H 49, Revolution is **H 33, Retreat,** with 1 mark (Fig. 7.26), so line 1 offers guidance on passing through the last period of change, in preparation for a new 'revolution.'

Figure 7.26:

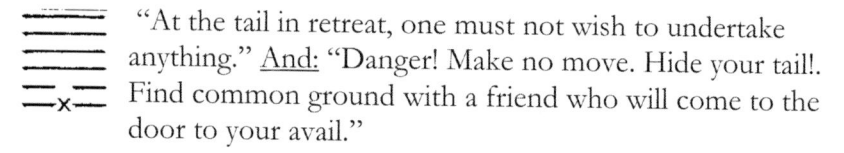

"At the tail in retreat, one must not wish to undertake anything." <u>And</u>: "Danger! Make no move. Hide your tail!. Find common ground with a friend who will come to the door to your avail."

Both sources echo each other in tone. The 'gifts' of these Interim Hexagrams verses encouraged our seeker to cultivate a peaceful heart and calm mind; to notice clues in the situation and trust a friend who offers support. These messages were an extra dimension for our seeker.

Trioles in Reverse

We know T 2395 flows continuously in this order, H 49...44...41:

Revolution   Meeting   Simple

T **2395**   T **2038**   T **3757**

Figure 7.27

If we reverse the flow to 41...44...49, the marks and values change:

Simple   Meeting   Revolution

H 41   H 44   H 49

Figure 7.28

The meaning of these lines reflects a <u>reverse of the flow</u> obtained by the method used for the original question, "What is the best course to follow?" Running opposite to the flow suggests a backwards-looking perspective.

Thus, as one arrives at 'Simple', and looks back to 'Meeting' to discover how one has changed in the journey, this message applies:

> **Simple** line 4: "If a man decreases his faults, it makes the other hasten to come and rejoice. No blame." (Book of Changes). ***And*** "Illness can quickly diminish by sending a message to the one who will help him. Estranged son meets father acting prim. Sincere exchanges create a happy ending." (Questioning the Oracle).

Looking back on events, our seeker could find hindsight truth here, especially with a father-son bond. From Meeting, we look back at the journey that began with Revolution and the changes it brought:

> **Meeting** line 3: "There is no skin on his thighs, and walking comes hard. If one is mindful of the danger, no great mistake is made." (Book of Changes) And: "Peril is there, difficulty in walking straight, due to corruption. Wait! Keep firm and correct. Keep faith. Remain still as others do the talking." (Questioning the Oracle).

This reminds us of the value of correct conduct and good listening, as essential aspects of the meeting's success. From Revolution, we look back to Simple, to what was gained:

> **Revolution** line 5: "The great man changes like a tiger. Even before he questions the oracle he is believed." (Book of Changes). And: Does a tiger change its stripes? A change will be made by the great man divining it. Gathering brilliant men, ones who are fit to receive gifts and praise now to arrange." (Questioning the Oracle).

Our seeker could look back with wonder at how beautifully this verse described the value of consulting the I Ching for guidance. While the original question was a 'Simple' one, surprising nuances emerged from this process that led to a great gift – a 'Revolution' of new awareness.

Curiously enough, the differences of the Reverse Trioles yield the exact same three 'Interims' found with the original Hexagrams!

Besides satisfying our seeker's desire for insight, we can also generalize the relationships between the Triole and its Interim Hexagrams, as in Chapter Four, where we showed how Triole 49...44...41 could be understood beyond the scope of the personal question asked, to reveal universal truths. To generalize with the three additional Interim Hexagrams involving Un-Time is a new challenge.

We showed that the concept of 'Revolution' demonstrates a universal principle of cycles of movement, forming our basis for measuring time.

We also explored the relationship between 'Revolution' and 'Meeting', understanding that growth requires one to be willing to 'meet' with an opposing force, situation or person.

The Interim Hexagram bridging the Un-time jump between Revolution and Meeting is Joyous, which illustrates the importance of correct attitude as a prerequisite for success. In any new situation where one is embarking upon a change of course, attitude plays a critical role. If we approach the unknown future with doubt and fear, we set ourselves up for the likelihood of failure. If we approach an opponent, competitor or partner with a joyous heart, we are more likely to experience the 'meeting' as a worthwhile event.

The next change took us from 'Meeting' to 'Simple', implying a general understanding that once a meeting has occurred, those involved must return to their simpler lives, perhaps to carry out whatever was agreed upon at the meeting. Between these, 'The Great Nourisher' (fourth line) says potentially harmful wild forces can be safely restrained; thus, by restraining any potential harm that could arise as a result of the 'meeting', one may successfully reach a 'simple' state.

The last change brings us back to the first Hexagram, from 'Simple' or 'Decrease' to 'Revolution'. In politics or cases of social unrest, people living in a state of lack eventually revolt to bring about a revolution. Naturally, if you are content with what you have, you don't want change. We go from 'Simple' to 'Revolution' each time we begin a new day, going from inactive to active states.

In the 'interim', or time between these states, we 'Retreat' before advancing, pausing before acting, to be sure the undertaking is in our best interests. Rather than awaken with a startle and jump up out of bed, it is best to take a moment to gather your thoughts, to feel ready to rise to the challenge of the day.

In closing this chapter, philosophical and practical questions regarding Reverse oracles are fair to ask: How can the I Ching reflect **past-to-present** growth, if for centuries it has been a **present-to-future** guide? **And** how do we **apply** Reverse verses to our lives when the sequence of events linked to the question for which we drew a Hexagram **must yet unfold in time, in order for us to reflect back on them?** Good questions indeed!

At this point, readers may be glad that we **know** the answers to those **riddles**, so we need not throw new Hexagrams to find their solutions! And the answers are obvious and gleefully funny once you 'get' them!

To our philosophical riddle: the I Ching serves to help us understand the magic of polarity and the natural harmony of balancing opposing forces of male, visible Yang / female, invisible Yin. Thus, the oracle's wisdom **must** apply to all realms of time ... ***past, present and future!***

As for our practical riddle, of how to apply Reverse verses, when at the time of the query events must still unfold: Since Reverse Trioles use **Psychological Time** or **Un-Time,** we see two ways to apply them. Our imaginations let us **jump** in **Un-time** to the end of an event, and look back from our imagined perspective, to see how we could arrive at that point. Therapists often employ this method in helping people to overcome phobias or anxieties, telling clients to 'see' themselves having completed the feared task or event, to look back in consciousness from that point, to 'see' how despite fear, anger, etc. they were successful. So too, in querying the I Ching, we can project our thoughts to the desired conclusion of the matter, and 'look back' to see how best to arrive at our hoped-for outcome.

Another way to glean meaning from a Reverse oracle is to **return to it after** the matter in question has played out in linear time in your life, when you can look back at how things unfolded, and let the Reverse Triole's lines reveal new insights about it. Naturally this makes more sense to do with questions of potentially life-altering importance, as it requires keeping a 'log' of your question and the Hexagram Trioles drawn for it, to be able return to them at a future time.

Because we recorded our seeker's question as an example, we **could** return to it years later, for additional reflections! That suggests that unseen forces delayed our publishing this book, to give the 'In-Time' needed, to shed more light on 'Un-Time' and 'Psychological Time.'

CHAPTER 8: TRIOLE SUMS

The 'Great Mystery' is: why is what is? We often ask ourselves how this or that came about. And on a more profound level, we ask how it all **began**. Modern Scientists theorize it as a 'Big Bang,' a sudden explosion of matter, out of what we would call 'nothing;' a better term would be 'no-matter' or anti-matter.

More recently, scientists have come to realize that indeed, the universe is filled with previously unrecognized and powerful forces that must be studied, which have been named **dark matter** and **dark energy**. These advances in understanding of our physical universe parallel wonderfully humanity's ability to understand similarly complex psychological and metaphysical realities.

Such is also the case with much of what we are proposing about the I Ching as an oracle, and how to apply these new principles. The general reading public was not ready to absorb this information in the 1990's, when we initially wrote this book and its prequel, Questioning the Oracle: The I Ching. We had to wait until the twenty-first century to bring them to a broader group of seekers!

Chinese philosophers on the same train of thought must have reached conclusions for which the great masses of uneducated people were not ready, and so they left it in a symbolic form to be developed by later generations. Fortunately, some of it survived the wear and tear of the ages and is discernable in the I Ching philosophy.

The Chinese called that state of which we cannot know anything *'Wu,'* and they drew a dotted circle, which they called 'wu-chi' (Fig. 8.1). Out of 'wu-chi' emerged the 'Universe.'

```
        ,-----.
       /       \
      (  WU-CHI  )
       \       /
        `-----'
           |
           ▼
         ( )
```

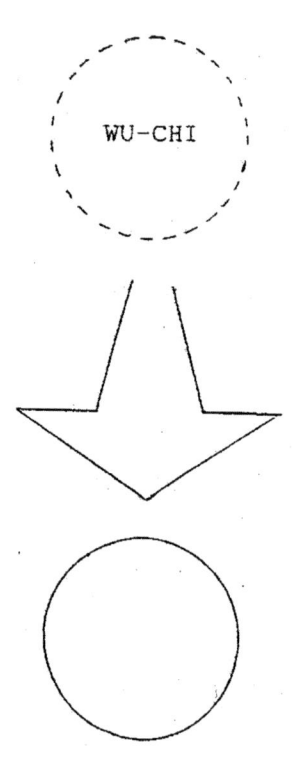

Figure 8.1:

On a psychological level of experience and symbolically expressed, concepts are likewise 'created' out of 'fragmented' surroundings. 'Whole' concepts suddenly emerge in exhilarating moments, wherein one understands the unity of the many interrelated phenomena.

In the next stage, two opposing phenomena are recognized, and were generally termed 'Yang' and 'Yin'. The interrelation of these opposites is shown in the well-known T'ai Chi symbol (Fig. 8.2).

The Hexagrams as they are developed are representing this stage, reminiscent of the bible story of separating the 'Waters.' In this context, the suggestion of some writers, that Hexagrams are 'Trigrammatic,' is not true. The mistake may have arisen by the use of trigrams to look up the 'number,' which is so mysteriously placed within the square. But, remember, trigrams are placed 'outside' the square as the 'key' into it, and we will use this key to open up other vistas of understanding.

Figure 8.2

In this context, the suggestion of some writers that Hexagrams are 'Trigrammatic' is not true. The mistake may have arisen by the use of trigrams to look up the 'number', which is so mysteriously placed within the square. But, remember, trigrams are placed 'outside' the square as the 'key' into it, and we will use this key to open up other vistas of understanding.

The next stage is one wherein after the divisions first were recognized, another division is realized, and these are generally called the 'Elements' (Fig. 8.3). Four were recognized: air, water, earth and fire. While we have evolved different concepts of the 'elements', the meanings ascribed to these ancient elements still apply in a psychological context. It was a major step made in reasoning and, as such, is discernable in the philosophical body of the I Ching.

In the foregoing chapters, we demonstrated that the 'step' went from Binary to Quaternary thinking, and was based clearly on a mathematical understanding of the step made.

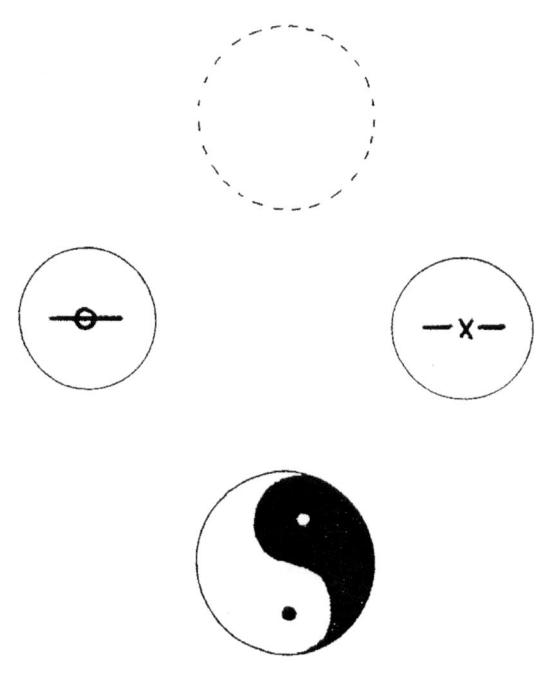

Figure 8.3

Again, the reconciliation of these diverse elements is shown in a symbol, which is also called T'ai-Chi. Whether the Chinese had differentiated the concept under two different names is not known. 'See' the images as superimposed on the dotted circle, as one could easily do with the modern technology of a motion-picture projector or computer graphics software applications.

Other branches or systems of philosophy, most notably psychology, also work with the four elements. And a wealth of so-called 'occult' philosophies, often called 'New Age,' also have much to say about the four elements.

In sum, the I Ching is basically a number system of two components, which we call today a 'Binary' system. To stop counting at the sixth place, for whatever reason, made it a 'closed' system of 64 images. Then it started on its way as an augury system.

In this respect, it is like many other 'mathematically closed' systems, such as Geomancy, or Ifa (solids used as auguries). Yet, what made the I

Ching a 'Superior' system, is that on the images is appended a body of wisdom, often cloaked in flowery language, already in early times, with the different Sages adding still to it through their age. The Chinese, in fact, never stopped adding to this 'body' of wisdom, as the concepts it carries still apply today. That the Mathematician was also still adding his knowledge to it, is above doubt but generally unknown, or put aside as too 'material,' too earthy.

Having drawn only one Hexagram, in our example, H 49, for which an amazing amount of text was already organized, why introduce a second Hexagram (Fig. 8.4)? How would this second Hexagram be deduced from the first, given that it had no changes? Which Hexagram would be the second?

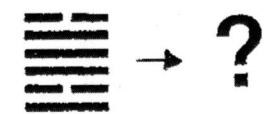

Figure 8.4

The mathematically minded Sage indicated the changes by giving a method to obtain the changes and put marks there to indicate them. It was probably left there, as uneducated lay folks could go no further without being disturbed or distracted from their purpose — to receive an answer from the Oracle.

These two Hexagrams (Fig. 8.5), therefore, signify: **What** and **How,** in response to the two main questions: "What will happen?" and "How will it happen?'

Figure 8.5

Although Sages kept silent on the **Why** of it all, one could discern or find it by understanding more of the mathematical import. History shows us over and over again, that underlying many a happening is a mathematical law that explains the 'why,' as we find expressed in the third Hexagram (Fig. 8.6).

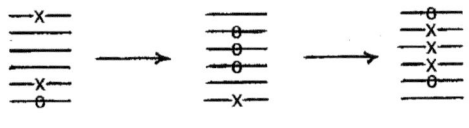

Figure 8.6

Yet, three Hexagrams are still an expression of Binary laws. Odd plus odd is even. And so on, as explained before.

So why should we use marks then? Because the people who generally come to the oracle need an answer; that requires them to 'read' the lines, even more lines, yet keep a tranquil mind and not be disturbed by their 'milling' thoughts. It suffices for that purpose. Those who become really interested in the concept of the **Why** behind it can benefit by going a step further and becoming mathematically involved, while remaining open enough to taste of the spiritual impact of the oracle. 'Spiritual' truths are expressed through symbolic images, as words tend to be restrictive.

Pressing on with this pursuit, we enter the world of four elements, whose basic law is: Two times two is four. Symbolically, you raise your vision above the earthy plane and start watching the Heavens. The objects that first attract attention are the planets, in addition to the more daily observable Sun and Moon. As the space surrounding the Earth was divided in parts to give it meaning, it also had to answer ever-arising questions. So, the Elements were combined in different ways to understand their import.

Early Astronomical observations became an Astrological art because of the meanings, which were appended on the Heavenly manifestation. It became all part of the inheritance of the Chinese.

Let us view our presentation of the Time-line again:

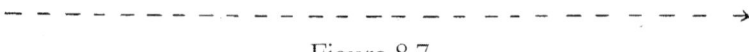

Figure 8.7

Let us now imagine that on the far left is the 'very beginning' or the 'source,' and on the far-right side, the resultant 'creation' (Fig. 8.8).

Figure 8.8

Looking to the left, we actually look back in time, the axis being from us toward what we see in the Heavens. In order to see 'forward", we must place the 'creation' in the center (Fig. 8.9). Looking forward in time very much depends upon what is observed as being past in time.

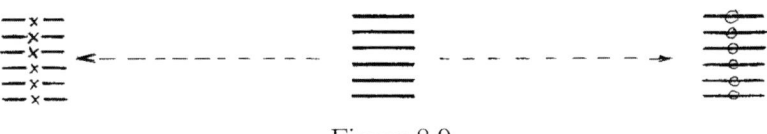

Figure 8.9

In the same manner, we look from a 'pair' of Hexagrams, forward or backward (Fig. 8.10), which gives us our forward or reverse Triole.

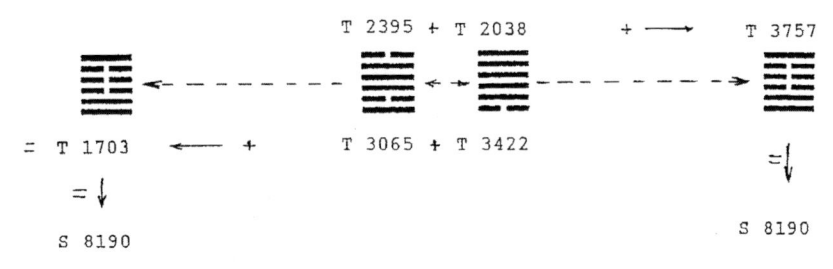

Figure 8.10

In this quaternary system, every Triole has a number in the set of 4096 possible images of six levels. The Triole numbers attached to this example are 2395, 2038 and 3757 for the forward Triole and 3422, 3065 and 1703 for the reverse Triole.

Both Trioles have these factors in common: The differences, which we named the 'Interim' Hexagrams, and an equivalent 'Sum' of the three Triole numbers.

There are two ways to apply this knowledge of 'summing up'. First is the Binary way of looking at the flow of change at every level (Fig. 8.11), resulting in one of three possible lines, in the case of changes: Odd-odd-even; odd-even-odd; or even-odd-odd. The remaining lines are always even-even-even, as simple as that, with Hexagram 2 always being the result.

Figure 8.11

A level with 2 odd and 1 even represents a 'moving factor', which we know from the Quaternary perspective. If we mark these levels and draw a Hexagram, then we obtain a center for our 'star' pattern (Fig. 8.12), from which symbolically flows the influences into the 'drama' and the 'power' triangle. This Hexagram is then on a smaller scale, the 'creative principle', as if between the ultimate source and utmost creation.

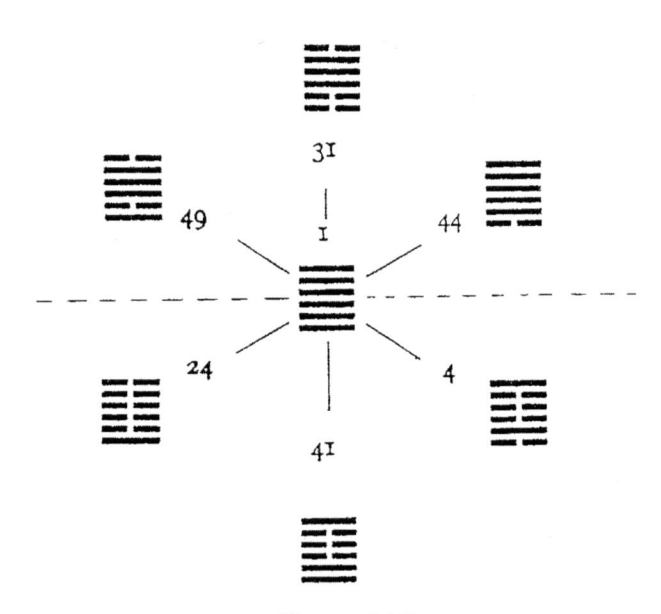

Figure 8.12

The example Triole had changes on all levels, and became Hexagram 1 with six marks, although not visible in a Binary flow of odd and even. In other cases, however, the marks producing the center Hexagram will vary according to whether change occurs on a level.

The three Hexagrams positioned on the Power triangle result from forming Trioles across the center. By themselves, the three Hexagrams do not, nor can they, constitute a Triole, but form a set, which we shall call a 'Tri-une', signifying messages from a higher level, the 'Utmost Heaven'. They operate with a 'negative' logic, which we will discuss further on in the text.

The second way is a Quaternary approach to obtain the 'Sum.' This results also in a fourth Hexagram, though not the same as with the Binary way. Symbolically, every Triole Sun is one point within a set of 64 x 64, occupying one of 4096 possible places. We call this the 'Greater Heaven':

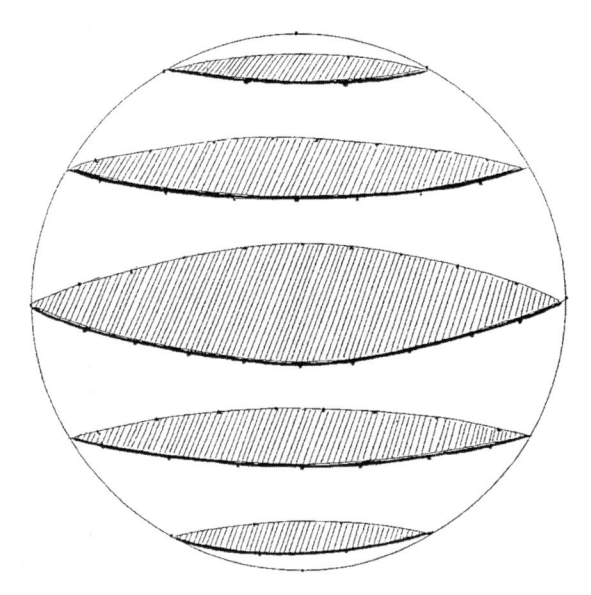

Figure 8.13

If a Triole Sum represents it as a 'whole', it is interesting to research the relationships between the figures, which then can be translated into an oracle. We start using the list that was prepared to sum up each Triole:

```
Triole Numbers        Sum

0  +  0  +  0       =  0    Group 0

1  +  3  +  2       =  6    Group 1

4  + 12  +  8       = 24    Group 2
5  + 15  + 10       = 30
6  + 13  + 11       = 30
7  + 14  +  9       = 30
```

These three groups again set a pattern (Fig. 8.14), which will hold through the whole set:

```
 0 | 24    24    24  ↓+6
 6 | 30    30    30
 6 | 30    30    30
 6 | 30    30    30
    →
   +24
```

Figure 8.14:

Let us call this pattern a 'Sum-Cell', and this Sum-Cell 0. There are 16 Sum-Cells altogether, the last Sum-Cell being 15. Sum-Cell 2 comes from Triole Group 3 (Fig. 8.15):

```
 96 | 120   120   120  ↓+6
102 | 126   126   126
102 | 126   126   126
102 | 126   126   126
     →
    +24
```

Figure 8.15:

Sum-Cell 3 (Fig. 8.16) comes from Triole Group 4, having the same basic pattern.

```
384 | 408   408   408  ↓+6
390 | 414   414   414
390 | 414   414   414
390 | 414   414   414
     →
    +24
```

Figure 8.16:

This basic pattern continues through the whole set of Trioles; with 64 possible Sums, some Sum-Cells are repeated to accommodate them all. Note how the number 3 plays a role in multiplying the Sum-Cells. The table that follows shows how often a Sum appears, once mentioned.

THE GIFT OF THE TORTOISE: NEW INSIGHTS INTO THE I CHING

		Sum			Sum
Sum-cell 0	0	1/3 x	Sum-cell 8	6144	1 x
1/3	6	1 x	1 x	6150	3 x
	24	1 x		6168	3 x
	30	3 x		6174	9 x
Sum-cell 1	96	1 x	Sum-cell 9	6240	9 x
1 x	102	3 x	3 x	6246	9 x
	120	3 x		6264	9 x
	126	9 x		6270	27 x
Sum-cell 2	384	1 x	Sum-cell 10	6528	3 x
1 x	390	3 x	3 x	6534	9 x
	408	3 x		6552	9 x
	414	9 x		6558	27 x
Sum-cell 3	480	3 x	Sum-cell 11	6624	9 x
3 x	486	9 x	9 x	6630	27 x
	504	9 x		6648	27 x
	510	27 x		6654	81 x
Sum-cell 4	1536	1 x	Sum-cell 12	7680	3 x
1 x	1542	3 x	3 x	7686	9 x
	1560	3 x		7704	9 x
	1566	9 x		7710	27 x
Sum-cell 5	1632	3 x	Sum-cell 13	7776	9 x
3 x	1638	9 x	9 x	7782	27 x
	1656	9 x		7800	27 x
	1662	27 x		7806	81 x
Sum-cell 6	1920	3 x	Sum-cell 14	8064	9 x
3 x	1926	9 x	9 x	8070	27 x
	1944	9 x		8088	27 x
	1950	27 x		8094	81 x
Sum-cell 7	2016	9 x	Sum-cell 15	8160	27 x
9 x	2022	27 x	27 x	8166	81 x
	2040	27 x		8184	81 x
	2046	81 x		8190	243 x

Readers need not fear so many big numbers, as they are easily brought down to proportion. Similar to exchanging a Triole number for a Hexagram, the same is done with a Sum number by subtracting 4095 wherever the Sum exceeds it. Surprisingly, the whole set of 64 Hexagrams appears, as you can see in the next table.

Sum	=	Hexagram	Sum	=	Hexagram
0	=	2	6144	=	24
6	=	7	6150	=	19
24	=	15	6168	=	36
30	=	46	6174	=	11
96	=	16	6240	=	51
102	=	40	6246	=	54
120	=	62	6264	=	55
126	=	32	6270	=	34
384	=	8	6528	=	3
390	=	29	6534	=	60
408	=	39	6552	=	63
414	=	48	6558	=	5
480	=	45	6624	=	17
486	=	47	6630	=	58
504	=	31	6648	=	49
510	=	28	6654	=	43
1536	=	23	7680	=	27
1542	=	4	7686	=	41
1560	=	52	7704	=	22
1566	=	18	7710	=	26
1632	=	35	7776	=	21
1638	=	64	7782	=	38
1656	=	56	7800	=	30
1662	=	50	7806	=	14
1920	=	20	8064	=	42
1926	=	59	8070	=	61
1944	=	53	8088	=	37
1950	=	57	8094	=	9
2016	=	12	8160	=	25
2022	=	6	8166	=	10
2040	=	33	8184	=	13
2046	=	44	8190	=	1

All Sum numbers are divisible by 6, as only two series of lines are involved. One line series, having no changes, is three, Yin. The other line series carries the changes, thus has an opposite effect. They are therefore opposite, like Yang and Yin, so we refer to these two possible line series as Yin-flow and Yang-flow (Fig. 8.17).

THE GIFT OF THE TORTOISE: NEW INSIGHTS INTO THE I CHING

```
     Yin-flow              and              Yang-flow

  — —  — —  — —                  ———   —o—   —x—
```
Figure 8.17

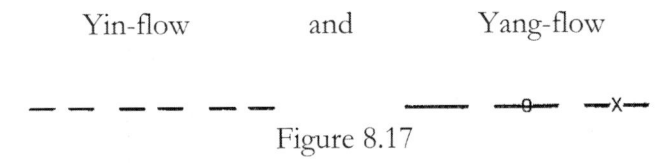

Yang-flow is equivalent to 1, 2 and 3 in differing order, always adding up to 6. Yin-flow is 0 three times, which does not alter the divisibility by 6. This makes it possible to have a key to find the Sum of a given Triole with only the first Marked Hexagram, such as it usually appears with the normal throw:

```
Level 6       0         6144
  "   5       0         1536
  "   4       0          384
  "   3       0           96
  "   2       0           24
  "   1       0            6
           Yin-flow    Yang-flow
```

The Sum is always one of 64 possible Sums, for example (Fig. 8.18):

```
T 2352  = H 39
 —x—         Second Column     6144
 ———         Second   "        1536
 — —         First    "           0
 —o—         Second   "          96
 — —         First    "           0
 — —         First    "           0
                                ————
                          S    7776  = H 21
```

Figure 8.18

This, then, is the second way of drawing a Hexagram for the center of our Star-pattern, which then changes the Hexagrams of the Power triangle. Thus, when consulting an oracle, there are two patterns from which to choose. For normal cases where an answer is required with a sense of eagerness, the first method, the Binary way, suffices and is easy to accomplish. A third Hexagram is easily drawn using the law of odd and even. By marking the lines having a Yang-flow in Hexagram 2, as follows, the 'center' is obtained, symbolizing the 'central' issue. Any consultant who desires, can also make the Power triangle as extra information by drawing across the center to form the other Trioles.

For instance, pick two I Ching cards at random to use as an oracle. No changes are visible, but a closer look shows that a line in the first is different in the second. As it changes there, the line in the first Hexagram should, therefore, carry a mark (Fig. 8.19).

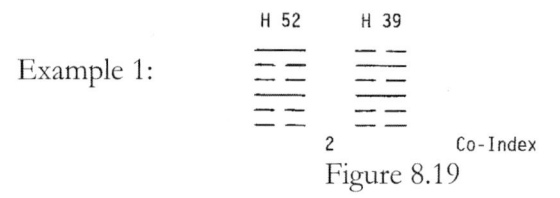

Example 1:

```
          H 52     H 39
          ━━       ━ ━
          ━ ━      ━ ━
          ━━━      ━━━
          ━━━      ━━━
          ━ ━      ━ ━
          ━ ━      ━ ━
            2           Co-Index
```
Figure 8.19

Adding the mark (Fig. 8.20) gives the same 'Co-index', so named by Terrence McKenna for the number of changes given by the usual manner of drawing a Hexagram.

Example 2:

```
          ━ ━       ━━━   <-  changed
          ━━━       ━━━
          ━━━       ━ ━
          ━━━       ━ ━   <-  changed
          ━ ━       ━━━
          ━ ━       ━ ━
```
Figure 8.20

From the example without marks you can proceed to make a third (Fig. 8.21), once you understand the odd and even principle:

```
          H 39      H 20
          ━x━       ━━━
          ━━━       ━━━
          ━━━       ━ ━
          ━o━       ━ ━
          ━ ━       ━━━
          ━ ━       ━ ━
```
Figure 8.21

By imagining the three Hexagrams obtained in a 'circle' it is easy to see another Co-index between H 52 and H 39 (Fig. 8.22). These Co-indexes are sufficient to point to a line to read.

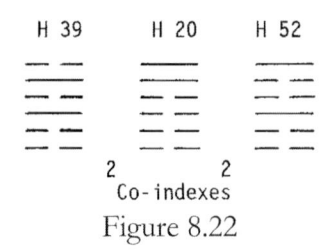

```
      H 39      H 20      H 52
      ━━━       ━━━       ━ ━
      ━━━       ━━━       ━ ━
      ━━━       ━ ━       ━━━
      ━━━       ━ ━       ━━━
      ━ ━       ━━━       ━ ━
      ━ ━       ━ ━       ━ ━
           2          2
           Co-indexes
```
Figure 8.22

Even this simple approach allows you to draw a fourth Hexagram to put in the middle. This fourth is always Hexagram 2, so you need not calculate, as one-even-and-two-odd is always even. Drawing across from your oracle through the center, Hexagram 2 always gives the same oracle you started with, so it is better to use Hexagram 1 as a center (Fig. 8.23), symbolizing the central issue of your question. Drawing across produces the 'Star' pattern (Fig. 8.24), which is as far as you can go without the marks but is already quite a lot for the normal asking of an answer.

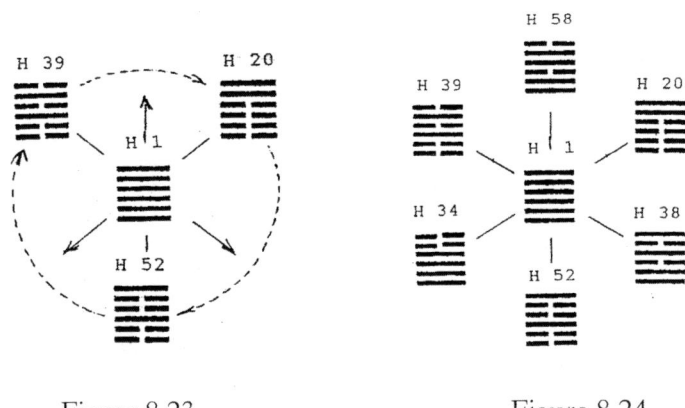

Figure 8.23

Figure 8.24

The question arises: why, then, bother with marks at all? The answer is simply that through the ages, the I Ching has given us a Quaternary system of changes, expressed with marks, that imply pre-existing Yang lines (Fig. 8.25). Example 2:

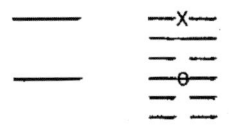

Figure 8.25

Those who delight in discovering the many intricacies of the I Ching are invited to see it as a quaternary system with a greater import than is usually presented. The Chinese were keen on numbers. Yet, more than mathematical calculations, we must stress that they also gave each number a highly sophisticated meaning that is unsurpassed!

Any number can be reduced to a Hexagram with changes, giving 384 beautifully written lines to answer questions; actually 512 lines, as for a Hexagram without changes, you read the 'Image' text and commentary as '0' line. Treating Example 2 as an oracle with quaternary consequences (Fig. 8.26), we discover, beyond a given 'throw', a grand spectacle of Hexagrams all involved in that throw. In Example 2, marks of the quaternary system are supplied. A third Hexagram then can be drawn:

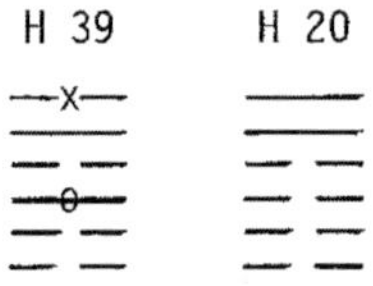

Figure 8.26

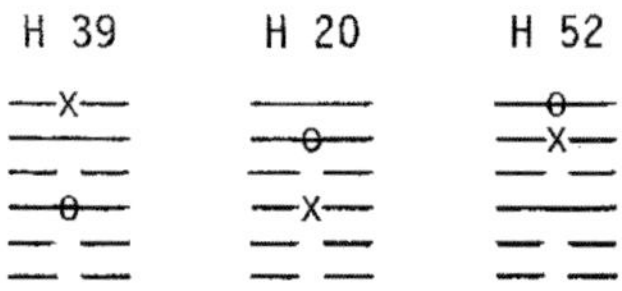

Figure 8.27

We check for their Triole numbers (Fig. 8.28), which we then add above them, shown in Figure 8.29.

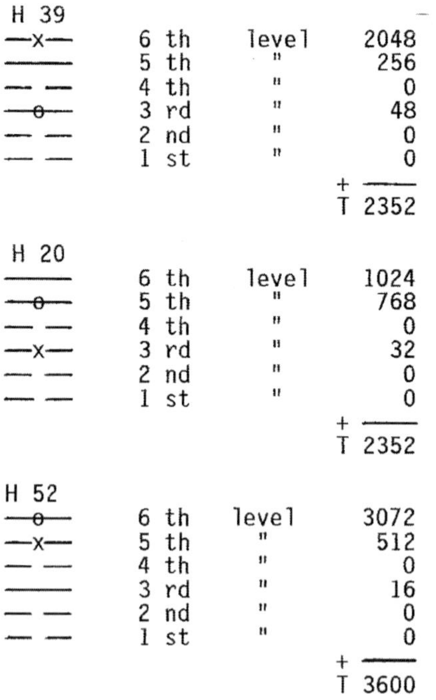

```
H 39
—x—     6 th   level   2048
———     5 th     "      256
— —     4 th     "        0
—o—     3 rd     "       48
— —     2 nd     "        0
— —     1 st     "        0
                      +  ————
                      T  2352

H 20
———     6 th   level   1024
—o—     5 th     "      768
— —     4 th     "        0
—x—     3 rd     "       32
— —     2 nd     "        0
— —     1 st     "        0
                      +  ————
                      T  2352

H 52
—o—     6 th   level   3072
—x—     5 th     "      512
— —     4 th     "        0
———     3 rd     "       16
— —     2 nd     "        0
— —     1 st     "        0
                      +  ————
                      T  3600
```

Figure 8.28

Triole numbers can be summed up and reduced to a Hexagram (also Fig. 8.29). For this you can consult the list on page 101.

```
T 2352 +    T 1824 +    T 3600     = S 7776     = H 21
  H 39        H 20        H 52       H 21       S 7776
  —x—         ———         —o—        —o—       - 4095
  ———         —o—         —x—        —x—        ——————
  — —         — —         — —        ———        T 3681
  —o—         —x—         ———        —x—
  — —         — —         — —        — —
  — —         — —         — —        ———
```

Figure 8.29

Sum numbers are an important piece of information. By reducing a Sum number also to a Triole number, you can find eventually the two other Hexagrams belonging to it. As show above, subtracting 4095 from S 7776 gives 3681 as the Triole number of our example Sum.

Now we can proceed to make a Star pattern. First, setting our Triole on the Drama triangle, which we call a 'Codon', and the Sum in the center, leaving out the marks as they vary according to the operation at hand (Fig. 8.30). As the Triole numbers also vary, so we leave them out too and retain only the Hexagram numbers.

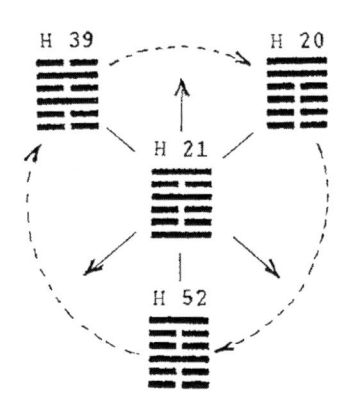

Figure 8.30

Combining the center Hexagram, representing the Triole's Sum, with our oracle by going across to form three new Trioles, as normally done, results in three extra Hexagrams on the Power triangle, which we call a 'Pokon.'

Using marks enables us also to obtain the Triole numbers (Fig. 8.31).

```
    H 39      H 21      H 13
    —x—      ——      —●—      2048    1024    3072
    —●—      —x—      ——      768     512     256
    —x—      ——      —●—      128     64      192
    —x—      —x—      ——      48      32      16
    —●—      ——      ——      0       0       0
    ——      ——      ——      
    —x—      ——      —●—      2       1       3
                               +____   +____   +____
                               T 2994  T 1633  T 3539

    H 20      H 21      H 17
    ——      —●—      —x—      1024    3072    2048
    —●—      —x—      ——      768     512     256
    —x—      ——      —●—      128     64      192
    ——      ——      ——      0       0       0
    ——      ——      ——      0       0       0
    —x—      ——      —●—      2       1       3
                               +____   +____   +____
                               T 1922  T 3649  T 2499

    H 52      H 21      H 55
    ——      —●—      —x—      1024    3072    2048
    ——      ——      ——      0       0       0
    —x—      ——      —●—      128     64      192
    —●—      —x—      ——      48      32      16
    ——      ——      ——      0       0       0
    —x—      ——      —●—      2       1       3
                               +____   +____   +____
                               T 1202  T 3169  T 2259
```

Figure 8.31

After calculating the Triole numbers, we can add the three 'Tails' on the 'Logon,' our 6-pointed Star pattern (Fig. 8.32). Having again no direct need for Triole numbers or marks, we leave them out. This Star pattern is an important symbol throughout this research and was indicated already in the standard square.

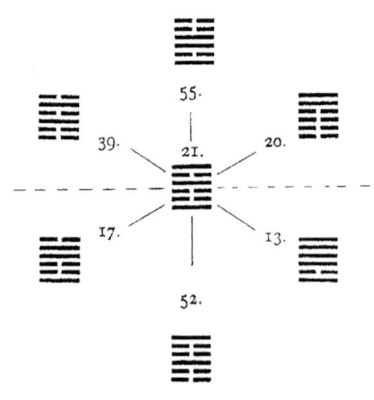

Figure 8.32

When the mind is attuned to a higher level, it wants to receive a message, which likewise has a high level of interpretation, not occupied with one's daily struggle and the questions arising from it. That explains why the Sages were also **Astrologically** involved, whereby their early knowledge of happenings beyond the reach of the Moon was, to them, Astronomy. We can smile of course, when coming across theories about 'elements.' Yet, they managed to create with it a 'way of living' for the 'peasant' as well as the high-placed official.

So, they left enough signs for diligent researchers to follow and to build further. One sign was the STAR. Seekers looked to the stars to find answers to an ever-questioning mind about the origins of the universe or how it all came to exist. They may not have reached the same conclusions as modern Astrophysicists, but they influenced and held together a large community. By following clues that they left, such as *changes*, **we** can change from a binary to a quaternary view of the I Ching.

Up to now, we have shown three different ways to obtain a 'center' for the Star pattern. The central Hexagram, being the fourth image, has a central place symbolically, as it signifies the **'When'** of the happening in question. When answers are required, and thus inspection of 'planetary influences,' the usual and most pertinent questions being: "When were you born" or "When is this or that going to happen? As this central Hexagram is placed on the symbolic Time-line, its proper function is to relate 'when' and point to 'five', 'six' and 'seven' on the Star, bearing messages from a higher realm, beyond the basic quaternary rule.

Let us look closer at that mysterious fourth Hexagram. In the first example, Odd + Odd + Even = Even, and Even + Even + Even = Even, thus the fourth Hexagram is always Hexagram 2 (Fig. 8.33).

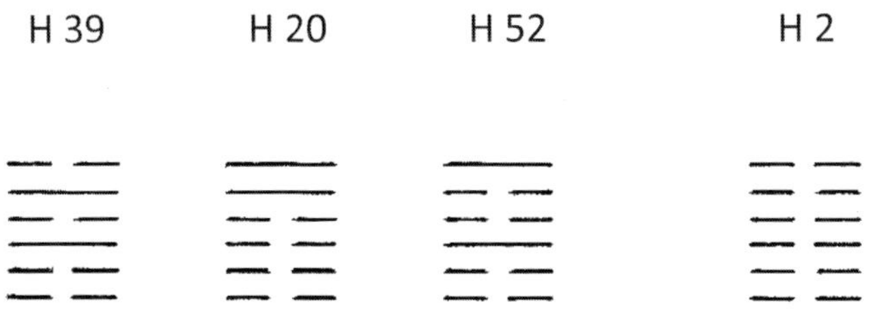

H 39   H 20   H 52   H 2

Figure 8.33

As five, six and seven, the Triole in the power position is a reverse of the original Triole (Fig. 8.34), giving a sort of backward view.

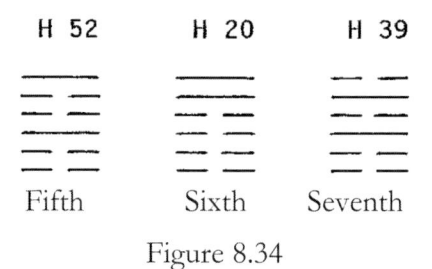

```
   H 52        H 20        H 39
  ─────       ─────       ─ ─
  ─ ─         ─ ─         ─ ─
  ─ ─         ─ ─         ─────
  ─────       ─ ─         ─────
  ─ ─         ─ ─         ─ ─
  ─ ─         ─ ─         ─────
  Fifth       Sixth       Seventh
```

Figure 8.34

This reversing of an original answer is much like the 'inverted' Hexagram with pairs, showing the difference in stepping up or down in the flow of time. Hexagram 1 in the center produces 3 other Hexagrams as a second way of drawing a Star pattern. Each Tail line is opposite its Head in polarity, placed in the Pokon, as were the reverse Hexagrams (Fig. 8.35.)

```
   H 58        H 34        H 38
  ─ ─         ─────       ─ ─
  ─────       ─ ─         ─────
  ─────       ─ ─         ─ ─
  ─ ─         ─────       ─────
  ─────       ─────       ─ ─
  ─────       ─────       ─────
  Fifth       Sixth       Seventh
```

Figure 8.35

These Hexagrams, being opposites of the Hexagrams of the original Triole, deliver an opposite message, balancing the mind so that it does not lose itself in a one-sided thinking process. Hexagram 1 embraces the issue in a balanced way, as creation is vast enough to contain the whole scale of possibilities.

These two ways of drawing seven Hexagrams are easy and open for anyone who does not use marks. Checking for a Co-index will point to the lines to read. We suggest setting a little mark beside the Hexagram (Fig. 8.36), so as not to confuse it with the Triole changes. You can read all seven lines, one after another. The law of seven pervades the whole structure of the I Ching.

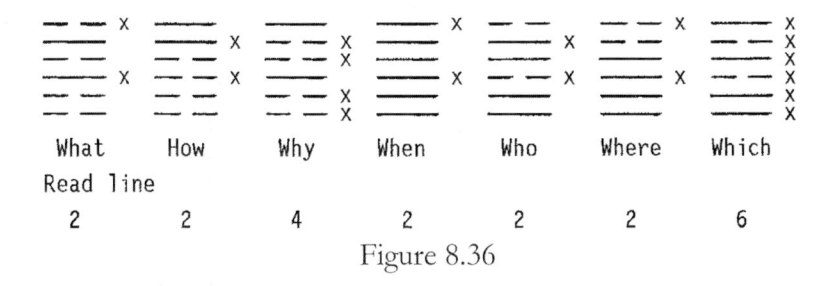

```
— — x   ———     ———     ———  x  — —     — — x  ———   x
———     ———  x  — — x   ———     ———  x  — —     — — x
— —     — —     — — x   ———     ———     ———     ———   x
———  x  — — x   ———     ———  x  — — x   ———  x  — — x
— —     — —     — — x   ———     ———     ———     ———   x
———     ———     — — x   ———     ———     ———     ———   x
What    How     Why     When    Who     Where   Which
Read line
 2       2       4       2       2       2       6
```

Figure 8.36

An interesting feature of this pattern is that while the lines of the Power triangle, or Pokon, 'mirror' the lines of the Drama triangle, or 'Codon', around the central figure of Hexagram 1, its Hexagrams do not form a Triole together.

That's where the 'magic' of the quaternary approach starts. We must now recognize the Triole as being a Yin manifestation within a much bigger Whole, which is, by contrast, Yang in essence.

The Triole and Sum numbers are a key into this understanding. If we separate the four last additions, taking them out of the Star pattern (Fig. 8.37), we can more clearly see that the Codon and Pokon are of opposite values, symbolically speaking.

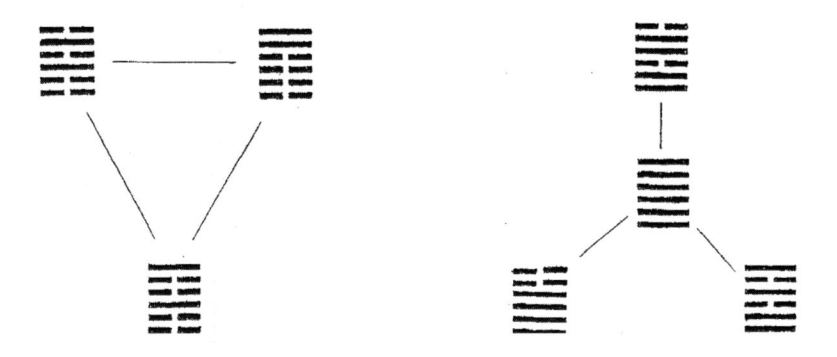

Figure 8.37

Sum numbers have a special relation with each other as shown in the Sum-cells. This illustration (Fig. 8.38) puts them in a perspective suggestive of a three-dimensional figure, which resembles the background for the Chinese custom of making those typical round paper 'lanterns', symbolizing the source of 'Light'.

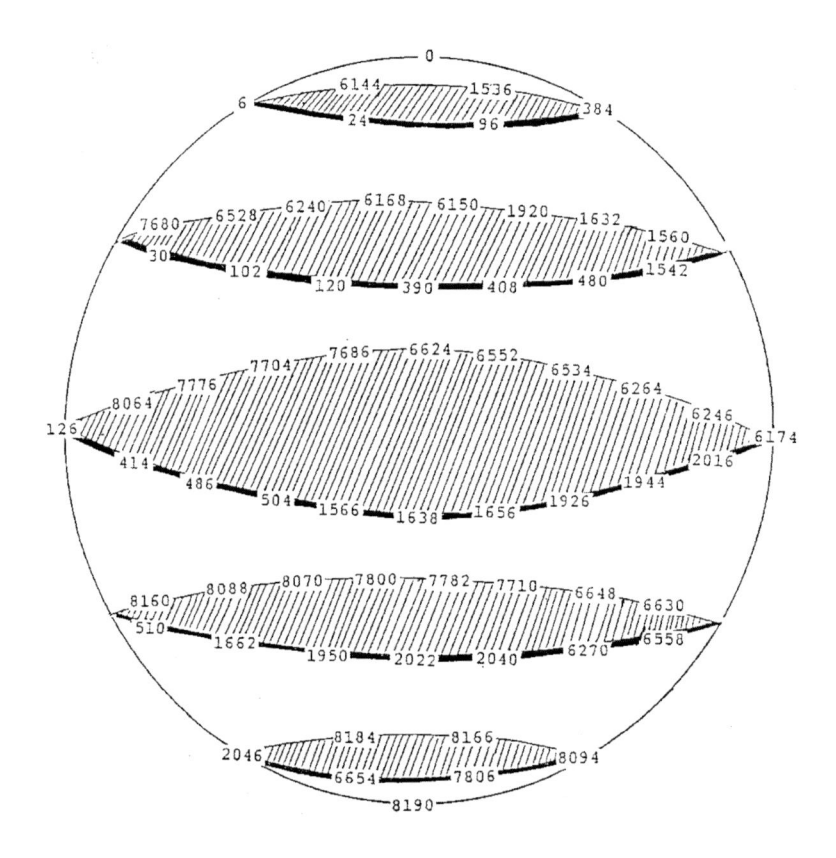

Figure 8.38

Hidden behind the I Ching's 64 images were 720 ways to go from 1 to 8190. Herein, we discover our Tortoise! We do not know if the sage Fu-Hsi discovered 720 lines on his tortoise or if he was aware of the quaternary significance.

As a closed circuit of numbers, many interesting relationships exist between each number, as with any set of numbers. For us, it means there are many relationships between the different Hexagrams, as each number — Sum or any other — can be reduced to a Hexagram. That will give a much more intricate view of these mysterious looking images.

(Amy here): I originally drew the turtle image below in 1970, when I found myself captivated by the patterns on my then-pet turtle's shell (Fig. 8.39). The actual drawing is about six times this size, and this was roughly a year before my visit to Amsterdam, Holland, where Jo and I met and enjoyed a summer of rare spiritual exchanges. I had stored this drawing in my attic for decades and only rediscovered it as we were first collaborating on this book in 1996. Around that time, by quirk of fate, I discovered a huge **real** Tortoise Shell by a vernal pond near my home, where the shell was abandoned by its wearer. It is truly a marvel to us, how tortoise-like this book sat quietly unpublished, for another fifteen years; a tribute to nature's mysterious cosmic clock.

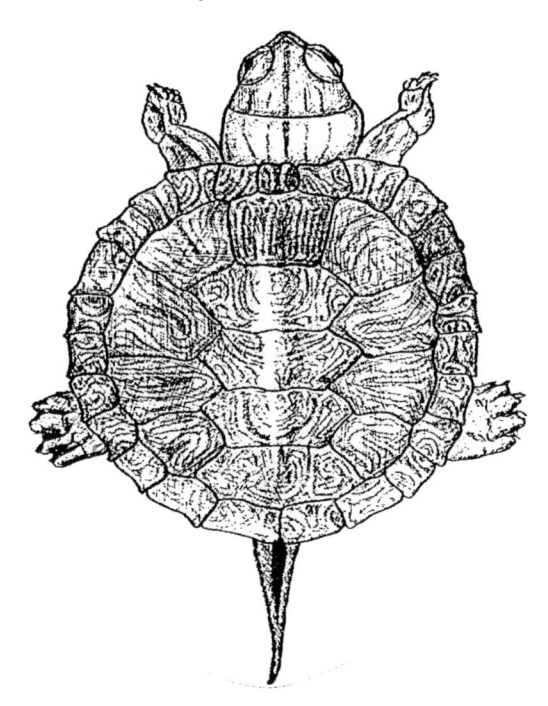

Figure 8.39

JO ONVLEE AND AMY SHAPIRO

THE 720 WAYS OF SUM NUMBERS FROM 0 TO 8190

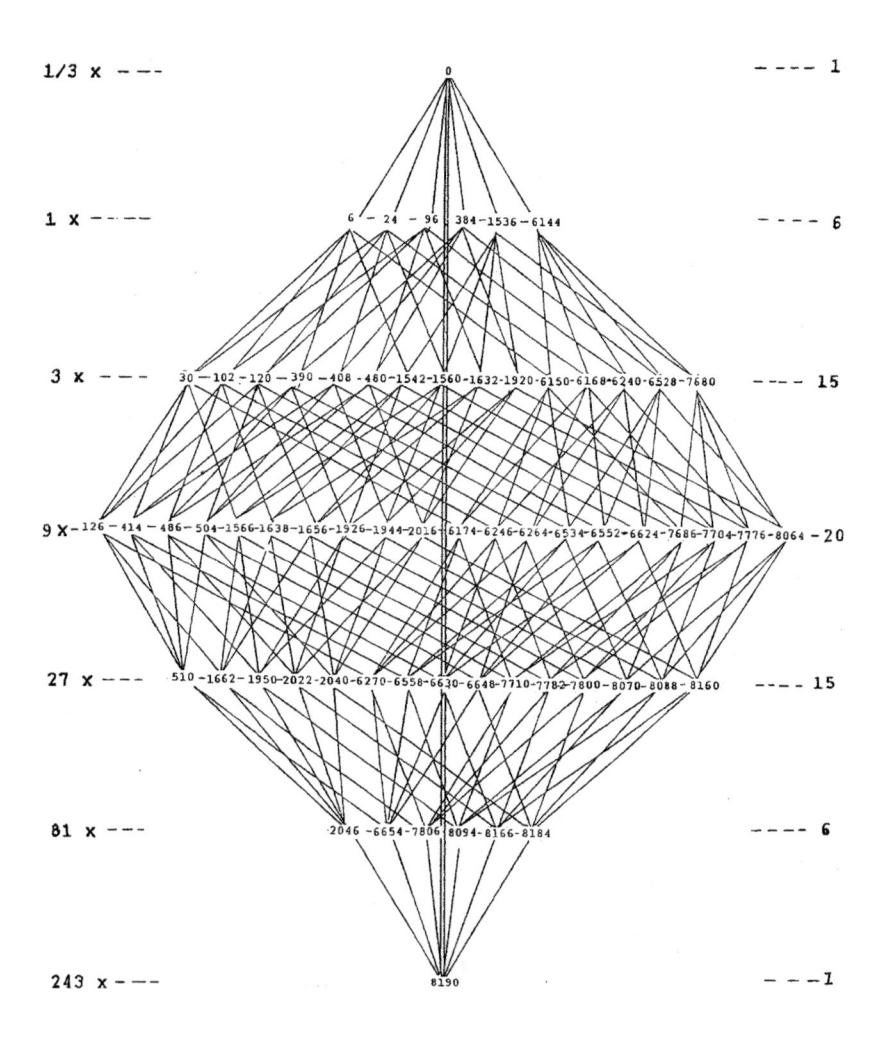

Figure 8.40

THE GIFT OF THE TORTOISE: NEW INSIGHTS INTO THE I CHING

720 WAYS FROM THE DEEP UNKNOWN TO CREATIVITY

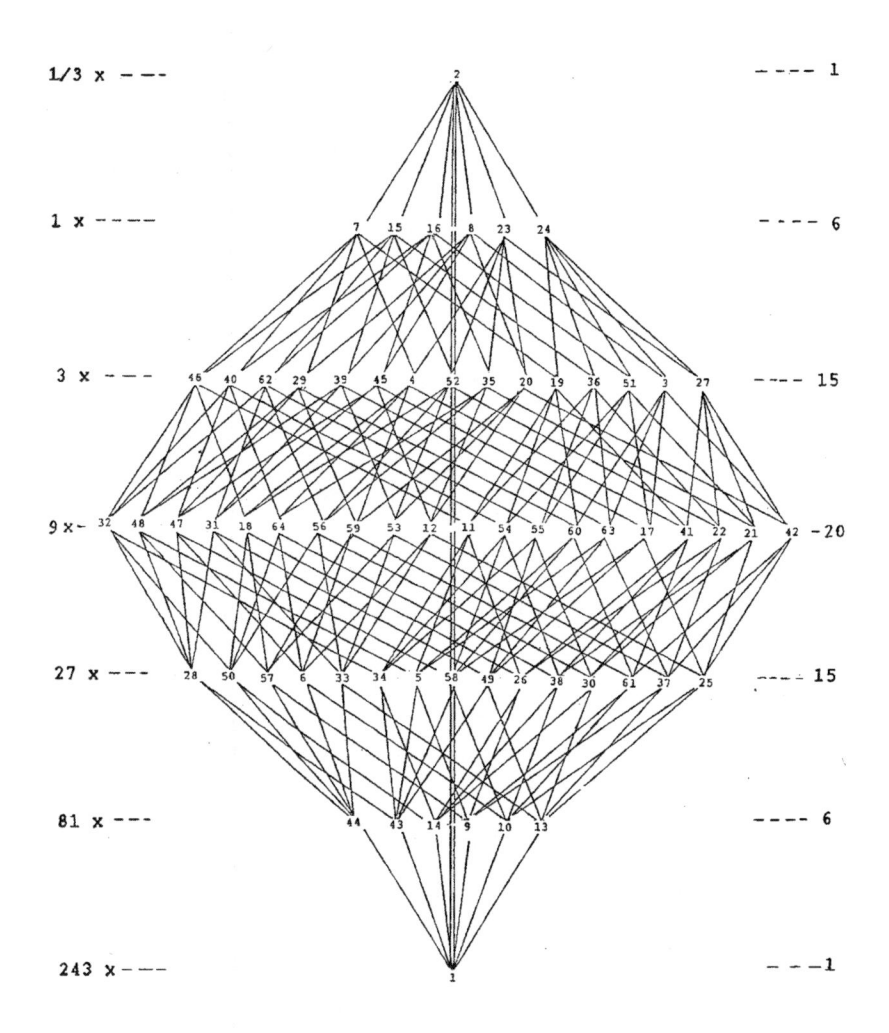

Figure 8.41

The tortoise figure shows the Sum numbers in relation to the different 'planes' (Fig. 8.40). The second plate (Fig. 8.41) shows the Hexagrams in their place. Remember, these Hexagrams are Quaternary equivalences;

each can sit as an 'Emperor' in the oracle's center. The 'lantern' shows each Emperor has its place on a certain plane (Fig. 8.42).

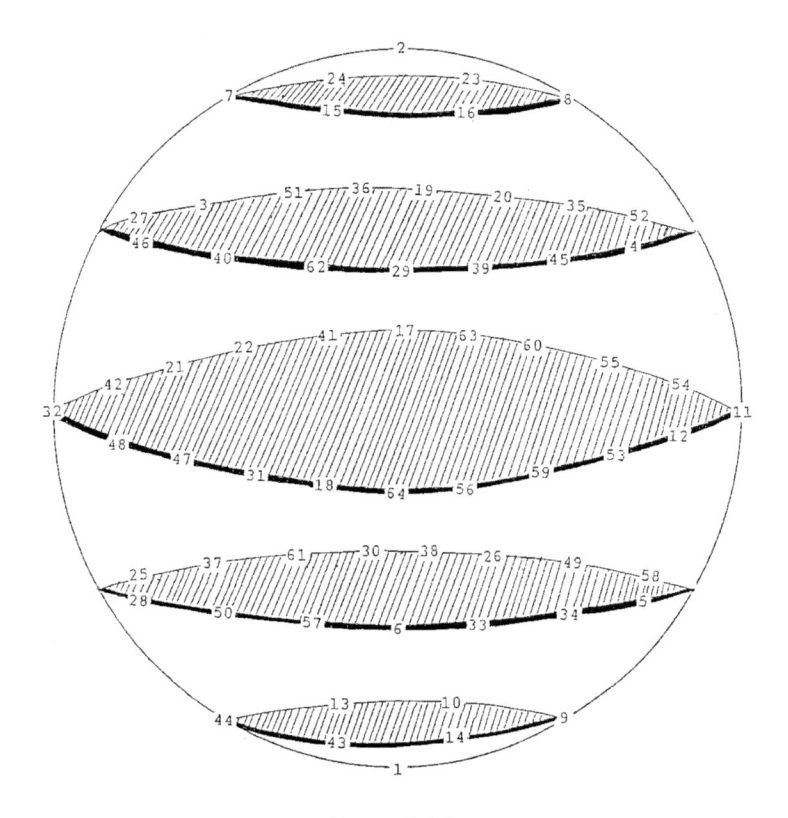

Figure 8.42:

As shown in Example 2, H 21 was the 'Emperor' and mirroring the message from above, with five, six and seven (Fig. 8.43).

Figure 8.43

CHAPTER 9: TRI-UNE TRIPLETS AND THE EMPEROR

With the fourth Hexagram, you can always obtain the next three by drawing a Triole across the center. The resulting Hexagrams do not form a Triole. They are called a 'Tri-une', as they form together a different 'unity' than with the ordinary Odd/Even Rule.

As we deal now with a 'Tri-une', we need to apply 'negative' logic. This is not as difficult as it sounds. It means that the normal response in a Triole now gives an 'opposite response.

— —	— —	Instead of Yin, becomes	———
— —	———	Instead of Yang, becomes Yin	— —
———	— —	Instead of Yang, becomes Yin	— —
———	———	Instead of Yin, becomes Yang	———

This is so because of an Octonary base behind it all (Fig. 9.1), not yet losing its bond with either Binary or Quaternary values.

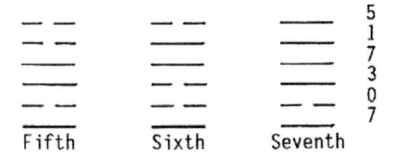

```
  — —      — —      ———   5
  — —      ———      ———   1
  ———      ———      ———   7
  ———      — —      ———   3
  — —      — —      — —   0
  ———      ———      ———   7
  Fifth    Sixth    Seventh
```

Figure 9.1

The strong relations of Tri-unes with the Trioles made us seek an 'identification' number. There are so many of them. Each Triole has a relation with 64 Tri-unes. This one is numbered 'Octonary,' to show the difference.

This Octonary number, 517307, is Decimal 171719. That is the step we are about to take, so don't be disheartened by the sight of these bigger numbers, as they are easily avoided in practice. It will lead us into a symbolic picture (Fig. 9.2) of the 'Utmost Heaven'.

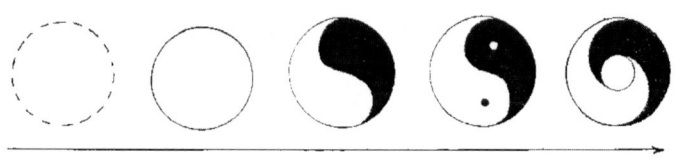

Figure 9.2

Normally, Yang follows after Yang, and then Yin. In a negative logic, after two Yang lines, another Yang line follows. In odd/even terms, odd + odd = odd. This is so because an 'invisible' change is involved, which we have called a 'wu-change.' While the I Ching is silent on this subject, it attracts much attention to the eight Trigrams, which the sage Fu-His supposedly found on a Tortoise shell. They are easily translated as the Binary numbers 1 to 8, and were always there to point to the 'next step', to look further in the sky. The ancient Chinese had a picture for it, which they called the 'third' step, the T'ai Chi Tu. It was especially used within the circle of EIGHT Trigrams (Fig. 9.2). Mostly it was preserved as a 'charm' against 'evil' influences that popular diviners could not explain.

THE EIGHT TRIGRAMS

Figure 9.3

The purpose of the T'ai Chi Tu was the calculation of times as related to the Heavens. That is aptly demonstrated in this picture of the spiral unfolding of sixty time cycles (Fig. 9.4) in Hua Ching Ni's monumental work on the I Ching, <u>The Book of Changes and the Unchanging Truth.</u>

To study these Time cycles, they needed to handle bigger figures, and yet not lose the bond with the Quaternary and Binary values. It may have been stated clearly and lost again, as few people would have understood it. Yet, very much is preserved.

The Spiral Unfolding of the Sixty Cycles

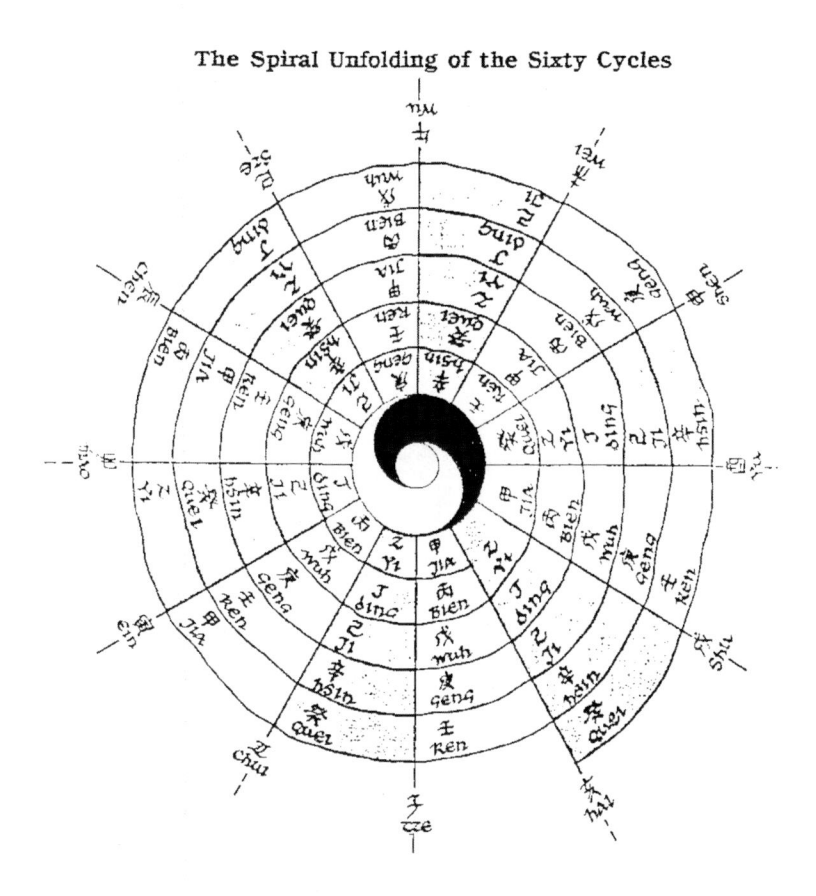

Figure 9.4

Most Chinese are aware that when they see the eight Trigrams, they are the numbers 0 to 7, although they are invariably numbered differently for symbolic reasons.

'Change' as an ultimate idea does not involve the changes with which we are confronted daily, but the more perplexing change of how something came out of nothing. The change from the Great Unknown depth to a 'Creation,' as our Universe is also called a creation. The Chinese call that source wherefrom this change arose Wu Chi, and the change from Wu Chi to T'ai Chi is an invisible one (Fig. 9.5).

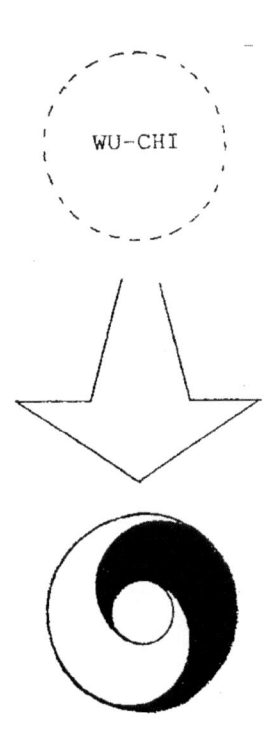

Figure 9.5

So, we meet in symbols of Yang and Yin, which combine to form 64 Hexagrams, changes that are fairly 'straight-lined' and easy to follow. With a Triole, changes go one step further, but still easy to understand; odd plus odd being even, and the quaternary aspect brought the number of possibilities to the square of 64 (4096). The next, 'third' step takes 64 to the third power (262,144). Expressed in terms of Yang and Yin, as odd or even, we meet with changes opposite to the normal effect, thus a negative logic prevails. This is similar to how negative particles behave, which physics now recognizes as critical to further understanding the make-up of the universe.

Our Universe, Creation, is the extreme aspect of what we mean by Yang, while the concept of Wu Chi is the other extreme aspect of Yin. **Creation means changing,** which concept is what we talk about with the I Ching. Even in its Binary appearance, it carries a key to these opposite concepts.

Let's review the process of forming a Triole, taking only one level. There are four different 'Triplets' (Fig. 9.6).

```
0   — —   — —   — —        1   — —   ———   ———
3   ———   — —   ———        2   ———   ———   — —
```

Figure 9.6

Each Triplet demonstrates the basic principles of what we call 'rolling and changing' (Fig. 9.7). Rolling, meaning no change at all, reminds us of the common saying, 'just rolling along' when one has no news of interest to report, good or bad.

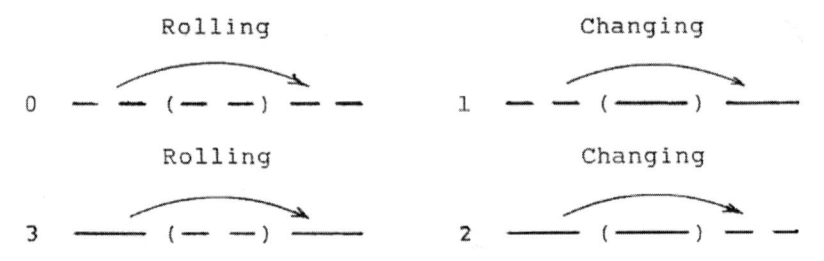

```
        Rolling                        Changing
0   — —  ( — — )  — —         1   — —  ( ——— )  ———

        Rolling                        Changing
3   ———  ( — — )  ———         2   ———  ( ——— )  — —
```

Figure 9.7

The one between the brackets acts like an 'Emperor,' causing **rolling** if Yin, **changing** if Yang. Removing the Emperor returns us to the four Binary 'Duplets' (Fig. 9.8) and Decimal values 0, 1, 2, 3.

```
— —   — —   = 00              — —   ———   = 01
———   — —   = 10              ———   ———   = 11
```

Figure 9.8

In the first case of rolling, Yin stays Yin. In the second form of rolling, Yang stays Yang. In the third Triplet, the Emperor shows its real talent, to change, creating something new. The Emperor as a 'creative agent,' can mirror the opposite quality. From there, it is easy to see that 'negative logic' is truly ***an act of creation*** in the Triplets (Fig. 9.9) that now follow.

```
4   — —   ———   — —           5   — —   — —   ———
7   ———   ———   ———           6   ———   — —   — —
```

Figure 9.9

Figure 9.10

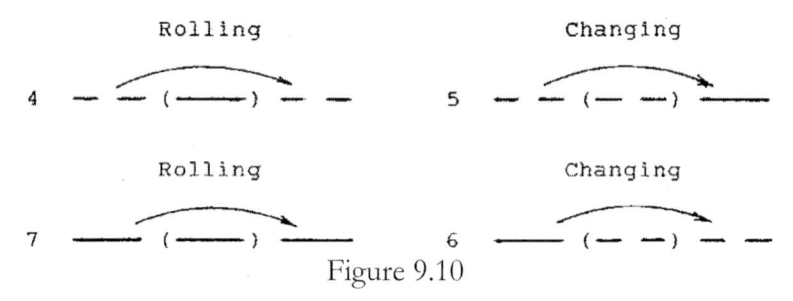

In Tri-une triplets, the action of rolling and changing is the reverse of what is normal in Triole triplets (Fig. 9.10). In a Triole, even plus even stays even, shown as Yin. In a Tri-une, instead of Yin, a Yang appears, because the Emperor stroke carries an invisible mark, which we call a 'Wu' change (Fig. 9.11). It looks like this:

Figure 9.11

We only need to understand the mechanics of it. The reason for this mark follows from the use of the other type of marks taken from a symbol (Fig. 9.12) with associative meanings of Heaven.

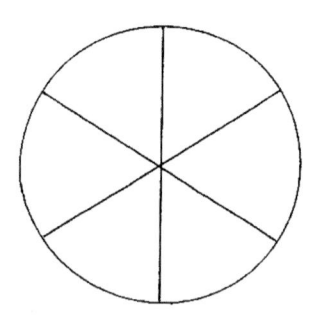

Figure 9.12

This mark represents the full Yang power of the Emperor, while the other line, fully expressive of Yin, remains invisible yet is nevertheless there as a Horizontal. Both actions have the opposite effect in the process of rolling and changing.

Here we see the four Triplets showing this opposite effect, which we call a Tri-une triplet. The flow through these lines is a Tri-une flow, as opposite to ones with the Triole flow (Fig. 9.13).

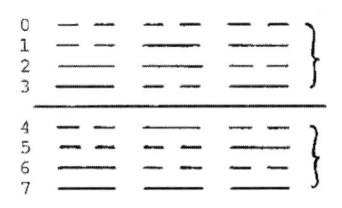

Figure 9.13

We have already discussed two special cases in Chapters 7 and 8. In the first case, using Hexagram 2 as a center caused every level of the Pokon Hexagrams to have a Triole flow. In the second case, using Hexagram 1 as a center caused a Tri-une flow through all levels of the fifth, sixth and seventh points of the Star.

We had set up a co-ordinate system of three dimensions and used as divisions on the line the 64 Hexagrams. Of course, as we don't really know the true order of the Textual number, we used a Binary order. The two first Hexagrams of the Triole, the Head and Shell, were set out on the front square. The third, Tail Hexagram, is marked in that big square of 64 x 64 (Fig. 9.14) by projecting it from there backward.

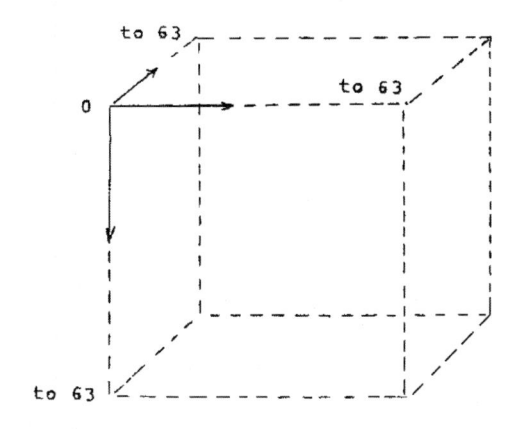

Figure 9.14

Figure 9.15 shows a Triole placed in a flat square.

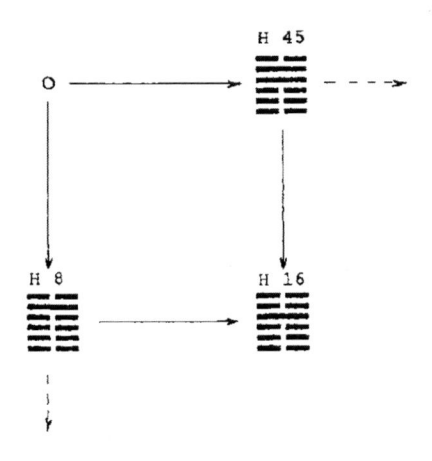

Figure 9.15

Figure 9.16 shows a Triole set in a cube.

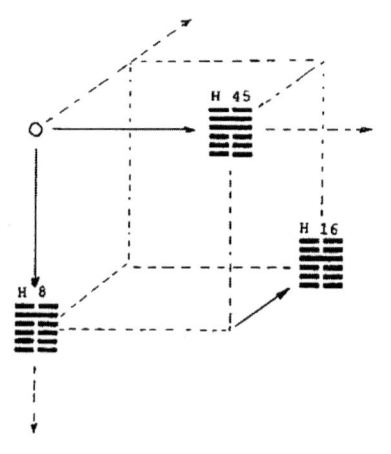

Figure 9.16

This model shows Triole 444 in its 3-dimensional relationship in a form that is like a book with 64 pages, each page a square of 64 x 64, behind one another, on which we can mark the 'Tail.' For instance, every Triole whose Tail is H 2, was noted on the first page, Binary number 0 being

Textual H 2. This marked out a diagonal line from the top left corner to the bottom right corner.

Making all other Trioles in their places gives us, to our surprise, the form of a well-known 'solid,' the Tetrahedron, our symbol for the 'Greater Heaven' embedded in a greater whole, the 'Utmost Heaven.' (Fig. 9.17). Of course, we cannot state that our Universe is cubic. No one knows the exact shape of this magnificent whole, yet, with 'pure' logical reasoning we may say "This is our universe, and nothing is outside of it."

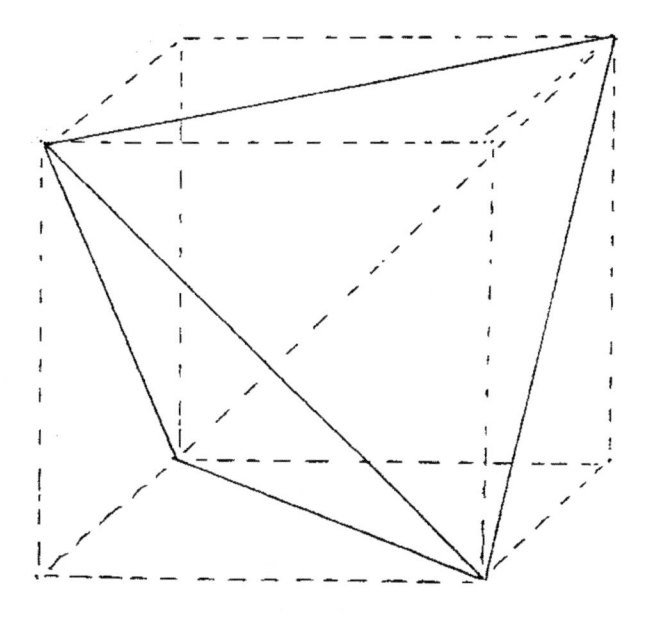

Figure 9.17

The shape of the five 'Platonic' Solids' have attracted many thinkers, and many attempts at a symbolic expression. Chinese philosophers also liked using these solids to expose their particular ideas.

We were not searching for it, but with so many Hexagram trios, a cubic expression best accommodates them all. There are 64 x 64 x 64 or 262,144 Tri-unes. Of course, 4095 of these are Trioles, which have the special quality of being a 'Family.'

There were other trios of Hexagrams with a special quality. When we placed Hexagram 1 in the center of Triole 49 …44 …41, in Chapter 8, to operate as an 'Emperor,' there appeared a Tri-une that had, on all six levels, a Tri-une flow: 31 ... 24 ... 4.

When we marked these special Tri-unes in our matrix, then appeared again a tetrahedron, but now from the opposite side (Fig. 9.18).

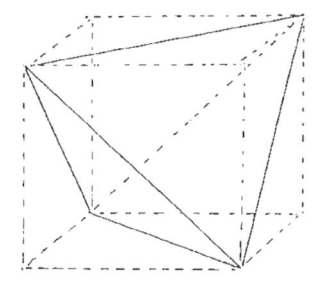

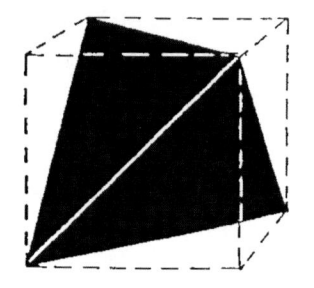

Figure 9.18

Interrelated (Fig. 9.19), they form a three-dimensional 'Star' pattern.

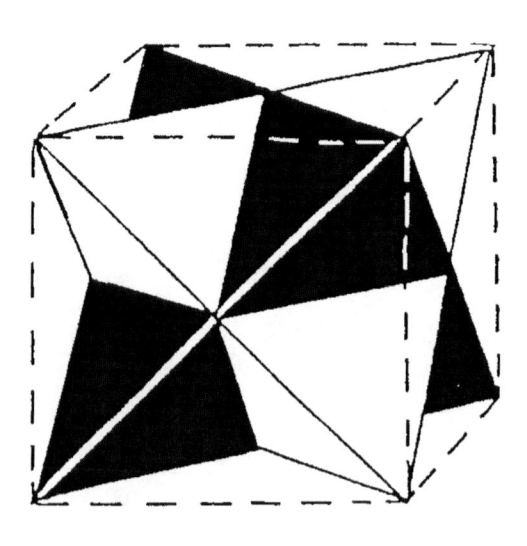

Figure 9.19

That our oracle's Star pattern also has a cubic form is evident when we turn it slightly, bringing into view the opposite of the center to show how the two tetrahedrons are involved. In this example (Fig. 9.20), Hexagram 48 belongs in the Tri-une space where the 'Family' is 'registered.' Sending its message to the Emperor through negative logic, Hexagram 48 functions like a 'guardian' looking after this family's affairs.

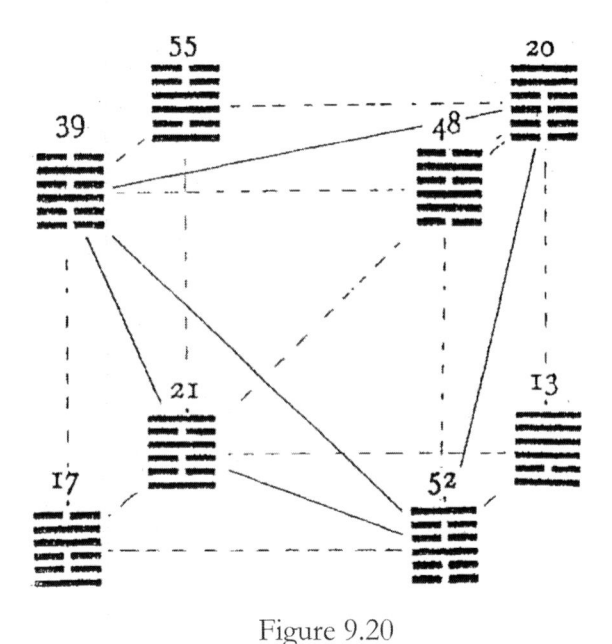

Figure 9.20

To clarify how we build up this structure, we shall use Example 2 again (Fig. 9.21) and follow it in detail.

Figure 9.21

Having already fully explained how a Triole is formed, we look now at only one level of the Triole – a Triplet (Fig. 9.22) – and we know that whichever one we take, the rule of odd and even always applies.

Figure 9.22

If this rule is 'opposed', then the third stroke becomes an opposite value (Fig. 9.23).

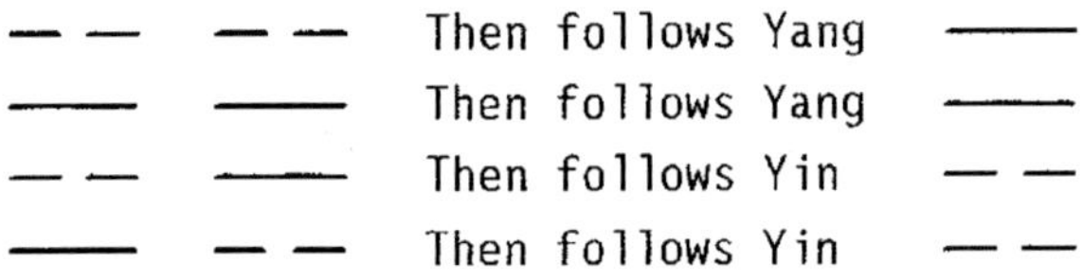
Then follows Yang
Then follows Yang
Then follows Yin
Then follows Yin

Figure 9.23

Then there are Triplets, which we have named Tri-unes, and the flow through it is a Tri-une flow. As a whole, a Tri-une triplet is an expression of an opposing logic. Normally, when writing binary figures, we assign 0 to the Yin stroke and 1 to the Yang stroke. In an excellent book on the I Ching, The Tao of I Ching Way to Divination, by Jou Tsung Hwa, is an example of the opposite way.

Therein he equals Trigram 'Chien' ☰ with the figures 000 and 'Tui' ☱ with 001. Correlating it with the Decimal figures 0 and 1 and carrying on like this, shows that his evaluation is opposite to the one we use. The one or the other evaluation is not particularly 'standard' with the Chinese or with western people.

It is important to emphasize that while we use opposite values, we use the decimal figures in a similar way; 0 stays Yin, 1 stays Yang (Fig. 9.24).

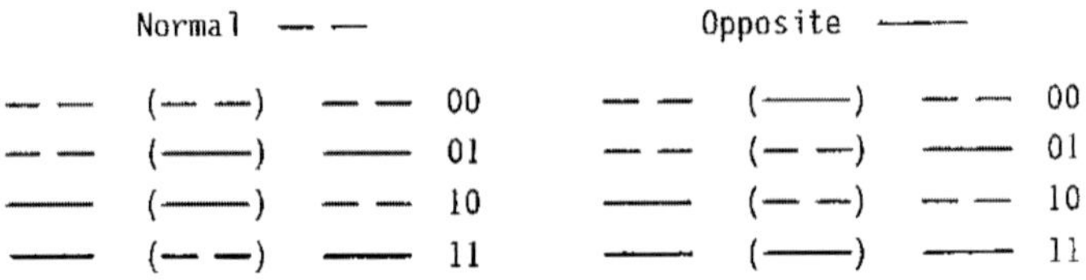
Normal
Opposite
00
01
10
11
00
01
10
11

Figure 9.24:

You see how the two different sets of triplets have the same basic 'elements.' The Emperor is the 'agent' imposing himself between or 'in' it and who follows the normal evaluation in one set, and an opposite evaluation – creating Tri-une triplets – in the other set.

The two sets, themselves, express a Yin and Yang process, whereby the 'normal' set of Triole triplets are under Yin domination and the opposite set of Tri-une triplets are under Yang domination.

The Emperor presides over the triplets, as the 'dominating' stroke.

Now, if we extract the Emperor and replace the dominating stroke with a 'Nominee' (Fig. 9.25), then we recognize the normal Binary sequence.

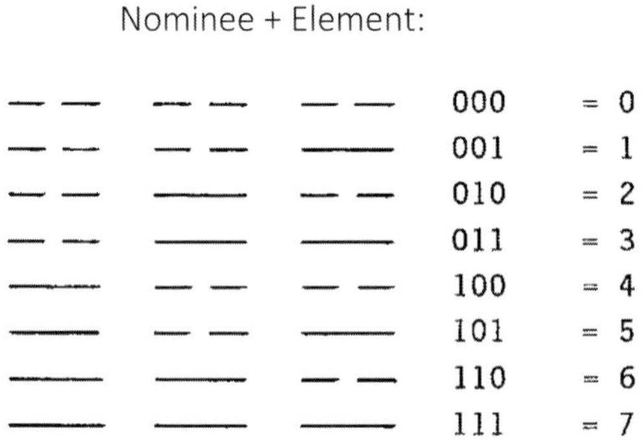

Nominee + Element:

— —	— —	— —	000	= 0
— —	— —	———	001	= 1
— —	———	— —	010	= 2
— —	———	———	011	= 3
———	— —	— —	100	= 4
———	— —	———	101	= 5
———	———	— —	110	= 6
———	———	———	111	= 7

Figure 9.25

These numbers differ from those shown on pages 117 and 123, due to the behavior of the Emperor, who displaces the Nominee. Therefore, the Triplets are numbered as follows (Fig. 9.26).

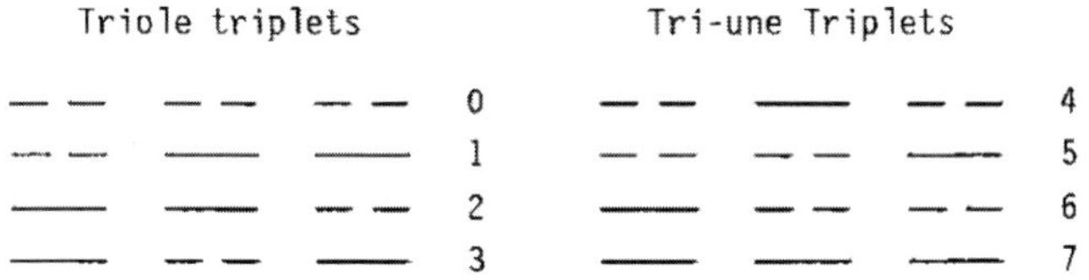

Triole triplets · · · · · · Tri-une Triplets

(diagram showing triplet patterns numbered 0–3 on the left and 4–7 on the right)

Figure 9.26

We call this second numbering the Triplet numbers, so as not to confuse the Triplets with the normal Binary evaluation. This code is strongly related to the four elements and the division of Triplets in Triole and Tri-une manifestations, used with Tri-unes.

Our example Triole 39...20...52 became associated with Tri-une 55... 13...17, on which this code could be used to give it a number in the big cube of 262,144 places. You can also use this code to find the Triole, if you started with a Tri-une by randomly choosing three Hexagrams.

When you desire to use these numbers to know the Head of the Triole, use the code and a complement of the Tri-une numbers (Fig. 9.27).

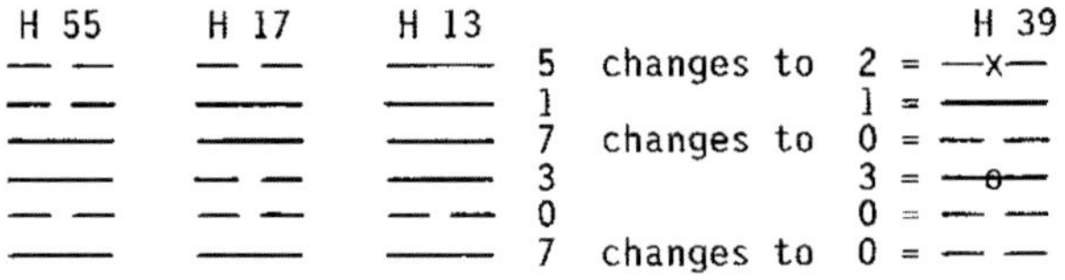

```
   H 55      H 17      H 13                              H 39
   — —       — —       ———    5  changes to  2  =  —x—
   — —       ———       ———    1              1  =  ———
   ———       ———       ———    7  changes to  0  =  — —
   ———       — —       ———    3              3  =  —o—
   ———       — —       — —    0              0  =  — —
   ———       ———       ———    7  changes to  0  =  — —
```
Figure 9.27

Triole numbers do not change (Fig. 9.28).

```
   — —   — —   — —    0
   — —   ———   ———    1
   ———   ———   — —    2
   ———   ———   ———    3
```
Figure 9.28

Tri-une numbers change, reducing to the 'complement' of 7 (Fig. 9.29).

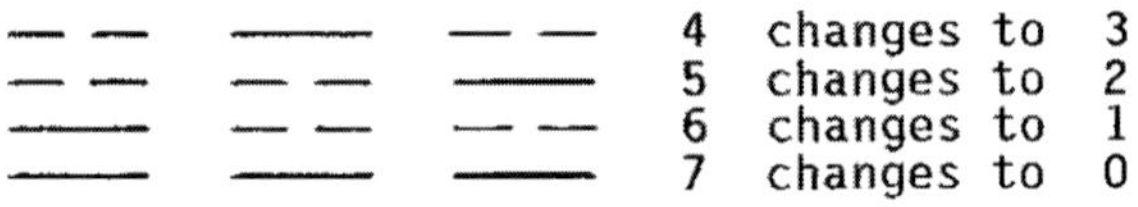

```
   — —   ———   — —    4  changes to  3
   — —   — —   ———    5  changes to  2
   ———   — —   — —    6  changes to  1
   ———   ———   ———    7  changes to  0
```
Figure 9.29

That is exactly what the Emperor does with a Tri-une; changes Tri-une triplets to Triole triplets and gives the correct Triole. A simple, easy way to find the Emperor of three Hexagrams is: count the Yang strokes in each triplet to determine each Hexagram line (Fig. 9.30).

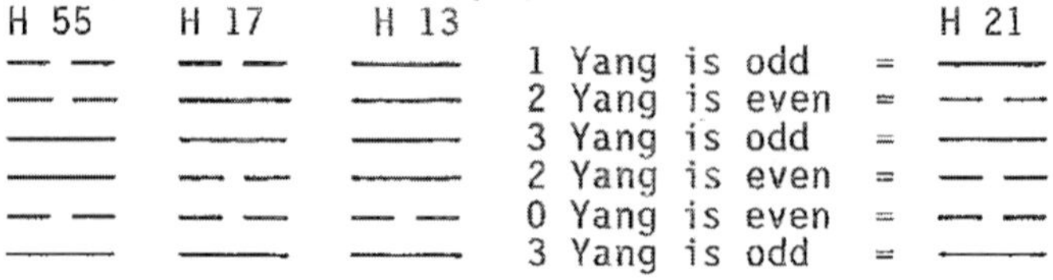

```
   H 55    H 17    H 13                              H 21
   — —     — —     ———     1 Yang is odd    =  ———
   — —     ———     ———     2 Yang is even   =  — —
   ———     ———     ———     3 Yang is odd    =  ———
   ———     — —     ———     2 Yang is even   =  — —
   ———     — —     — —     0 Yang is even   =  — —
   ———     ———     ———     3 Yang is odd    =  ———
```
Figure 9.30

By adding the Emperor to the Tri-une (Fig. 9.31), one can easily find the Triole (Fig. 9.34) from there, as the next three figures illustrate.

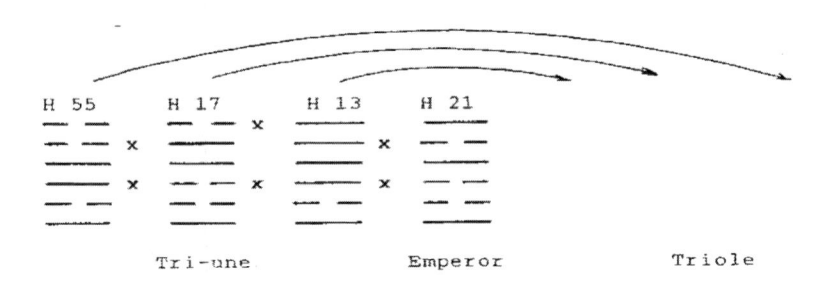

Figure 9.31

On each level of the Emperor, if there is a Yang stroke (Fig. 9.32), the Triole triplet mirrors and opposes the value of the Tri-une strokes of that level. For example:

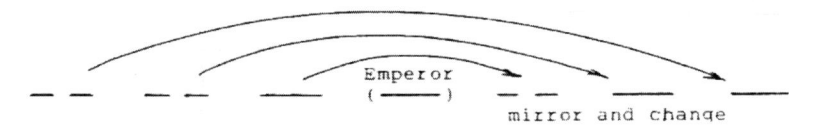

Figure 9.32

Where the Emperor's stroke is Yin (Fig. 9.33), the Triole triplet only mirrors that level's Tri-une strokes.

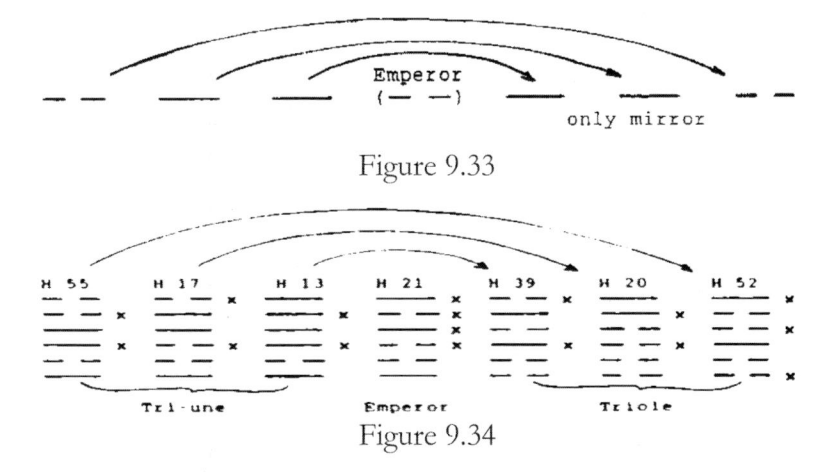

Figure 9.33

Figure 9.34

Normally, you depart from a Triole, for that is how a normal oracle starts. The previous explanation made clear that the Tri-une is so strongly related to the Triole, that the process could be reversed (Fig. 9.35). Perhaps, after all, the process may start with a Tri-une before the question even manifests, which needs an answer to contemplate!

That last remark is something we wanted to mention, as there is great value in not only asking questions of the I Ching, but in pondering the answer over and over, even to meditate on it.

Figure 9.35

As we already explained, the development from Triole to Tri-une, we shall mention here that an Emperor can also be known by adding up the Quaternary numbers of the Tri-une, just as with the Triole numbers, which shows how closely the Emperor is related to the Triole in question.

This close relationship of all seven Hexagrams is shown to be a three-dimensional structure, as we illustrated in Figures 9.18 and 9.19. Curiously enough, this cubic expression is often used with the eight Trigrams with various explanations. There are, however, too many variations, so we will set out to build it up from our viewpoint.

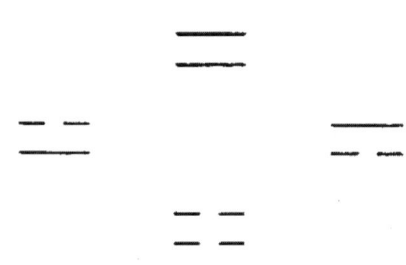

Figure 9.36

Of course, by 'elements', we do not mean the chemical constituents of the known material Universe. As with the Greek philosophers, the elements are intended as psychological properties and, as such, they are here discussed. The Chinese held closely to a system of five elements known as fire, water, metal, earth and wood. At the same time, the I Ching combines two different lines, Yang and Yin, to symbolize only four images (Fig. 9.37) as building blocks to be understood as elemental.

Figure 9.37

Various Chinese authorities still argue over whether ▬▬ is to be called 'young Yang' or 'young Yin'. This may stem from its appearance in the timeline as time quanta, where 'stepping up' or 'stepping down' gives the same image but is essentially different. Figure 9.38:

Stepping up

Stepping down

It easily leads to a difference in interpreting the underlying Binary code. Therefore, one finds in the books on I Ching both ways of reading. While they all build up a Hexagram from bottom upward, you will find many examples of the Binary code being read downward. Just check the 'standard square' for instance. To avoid mistakes, one must check first in what direction it is used. Figure 9.39:

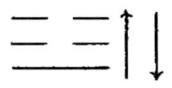

Must you interpret this as Binary number 4 or 1? In this discussion, we maintain that 0 is Yin, and Yang is 1, building the Hexagram up from the bottom; thus. what we call 'elemental' (Fig. 9.40) correlates with the Binary figures 00, 01, 10 and 11.

00   01   10   11

Figure 9.40

CHAPTER 10: PARALLELS AND A PARABLE

When in the deep unknown 'untime' it becomes 'decided' to 'create' a Universe, both Yang and Yin appear, manifested as the creative and its complement, the receptive principle. The 'Identity' created is like a point with no measurable dimensions, yet it exists. The further act of creation being the many shells surrounding that point.

Imagine the 'I' bolstered with many 'shells' and hidden deep inside is the core. As every identity has a number of shells and is then a 'being' as normally understood, four states are initially discernable: cold, warm, dry and moist. They are to be taken as intentional forces, like Yang and Yin. Though they are four, this does not yet suffice as to take them as the elements. Their force of 'intention' can best be expressed by the octahedron (Fig. 10.1), wherein each has its place of 'dominion'.

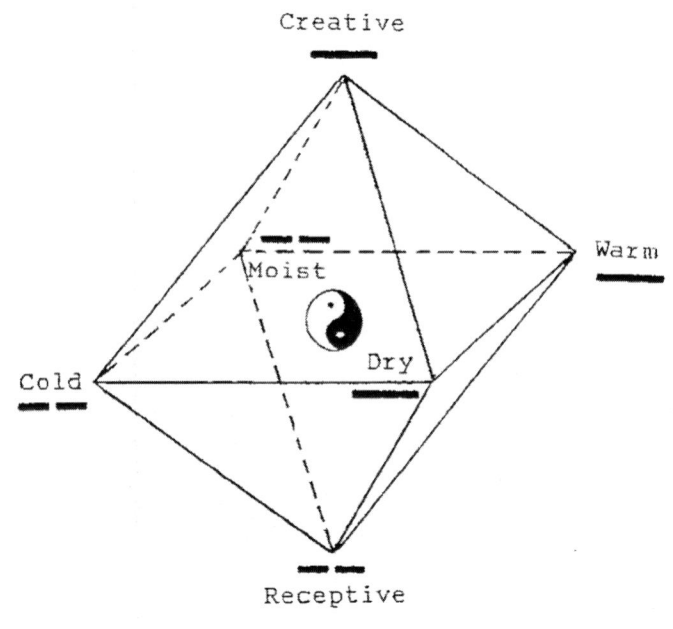

Figure 10.1

This dominion rests first with the corners, which are either Yang or Yin. Secondly, the lines between same signs have the same assignment. Thirdly, the faces surrounded with three forces of the same quality bear as a whole this force. The three forces coming together form the eight types of triplets, in their Triole and Tri-une expressions.

The 'intentional force' meeting a force agreeing or disagreeing with it, creates the elements. And elements are created on two planes (Fig. 10.2), on Earth and in Heaven.

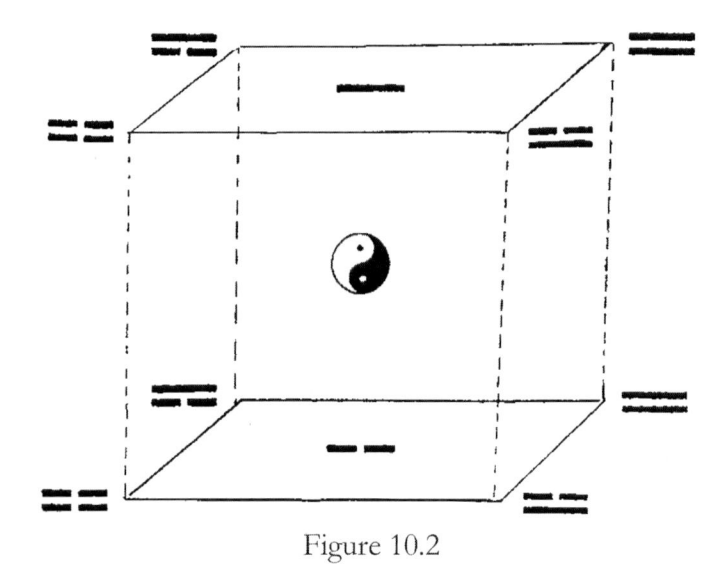

Figure 10.2

Between the two planes, the elements are again united in either a Triole or a Tri-une. The two tetrahedrons are each combining their forces between the two planes (Fig. 10.3).

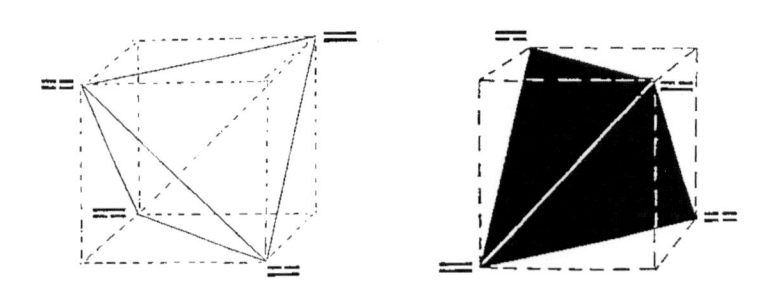

Figure 10.3

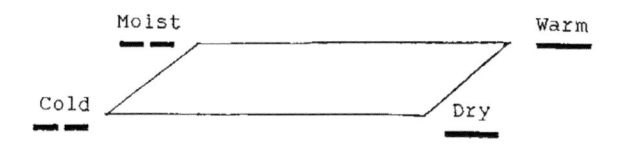

[Figure 10.4 — diagram showing Moist, Warm, Cold, Dry at corners of a parallelogram]

Figure 10.4

The intentional forces are like the 'Mutable' modality within astrology, paving the way for the 'Cardinal' elements (Fig. 10.4). Neither flesh nor fish, the intentional forces create the elements and are, in turn, created by the elements. They have a close relationship and keep throughout a dominant position.

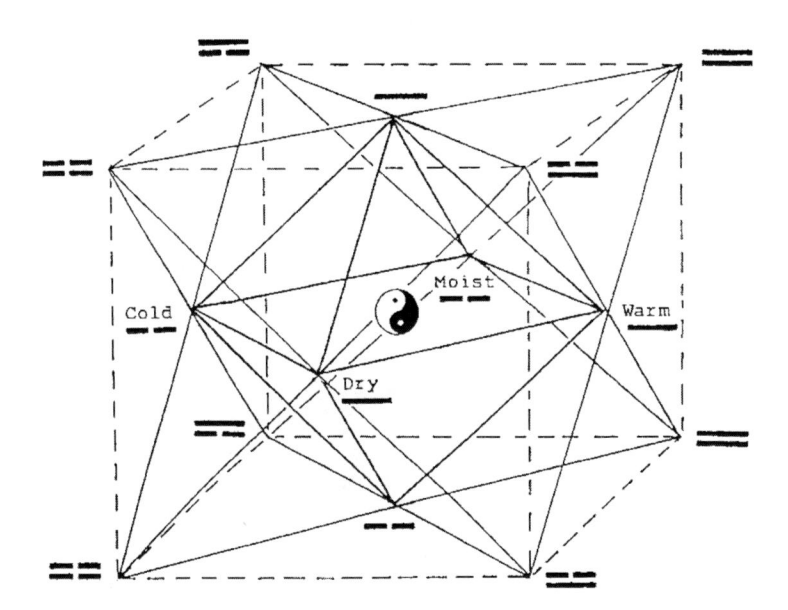

[Figure 10.5 — cube diagram with trigrams at vertices and Cold, Warm, Moist, Dry labels with yin-yang symbol]

Figure 10.5

The two main aspects of the creation, the creative and receptive forces, keep their dominion of the 'axis' of 'incarnation', of 'life' as a whole (Fig. 10.5).

On that axis, we place the Chinese element 'wood', to signify all vegetation manifestations on earth (Fig. 10.6). As an element, wood is life and supports life wholly. The other four elements take up their place (Fig. 10.7) in order to support life in their own departments.

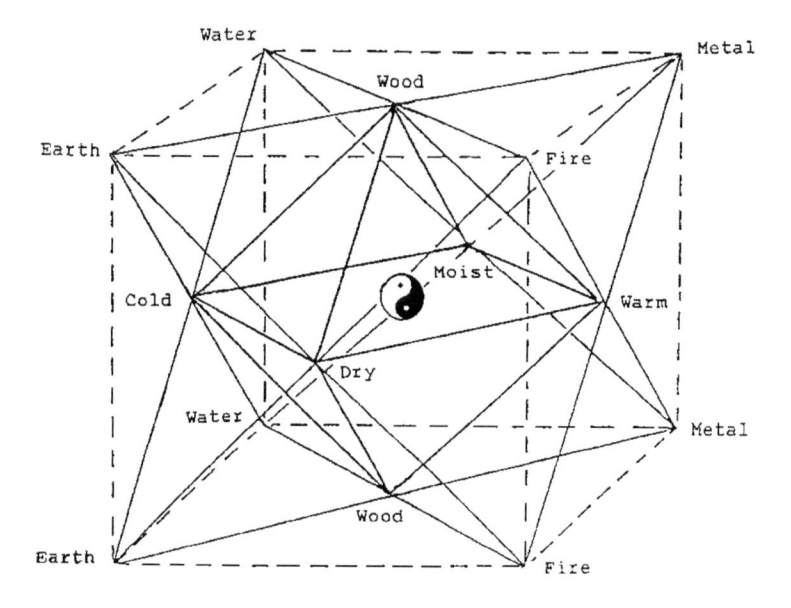

Figure 10.6

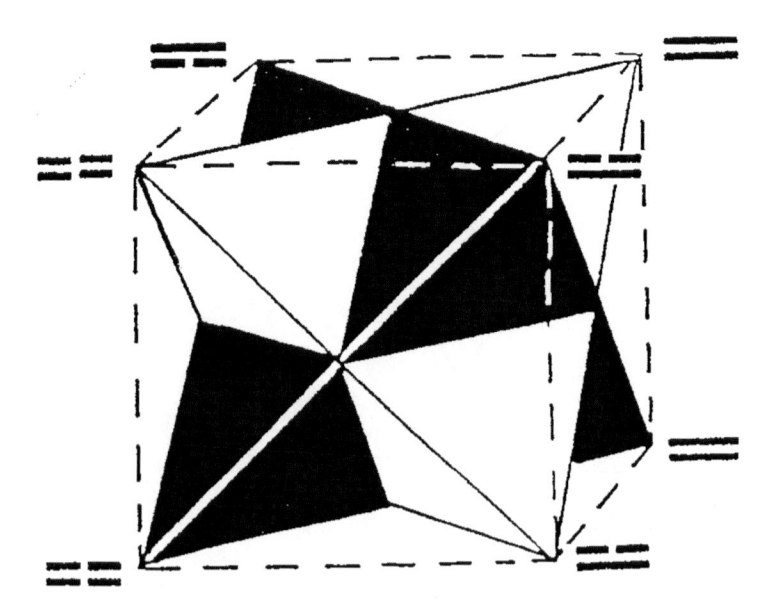

Figure 10.7

The Trigrams themselves are a step made from the elements by the action of the dominant force, the creative. A common mistake people make is to think the I Ching was created from these eight Trigrams. This is assumed so because of the need to arrange them alongside a square of Hexagram numbers, enabling people to find the Hexagram indicated by the oracle. No! They are created by the intentional force, the created, which takes up its dominion after a turn of 'events'.

This is easily shown by ordinary figures. If you write a naught or one, no matter how many naughts you put in front of it, it stays the same amount. 0001 or 0000. The very moment you place a 1, a Yang force, in front of it, you create a higher scale, which then becomes 10, 100, 1000 and so on.

In the beginning there was 0   − −   How? We don't know.
Then the 'Creation' started 1   ⎯⎯   How? We don't know.

That was the 'turn of events', which mystery duplicates itself endlessly. Each time, the creative and receptive principles take up their dominion as with the four elements (Fig. 10.8).

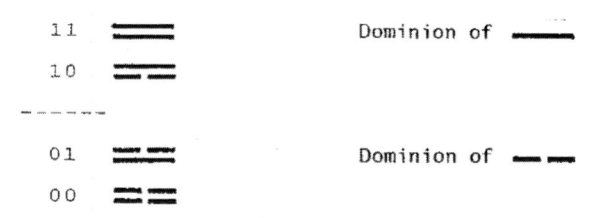

11	⎯⎯	Dominion of ⎯⎯
10	⎯⎯	
01	− −	Dominion of − −
00	− −	

Figure 10.8

The creation of the eight Trigrams (Fig. 10.9) starts after that by its duplication, and the two dominating forces taking a higher scale to 'govern' the process:

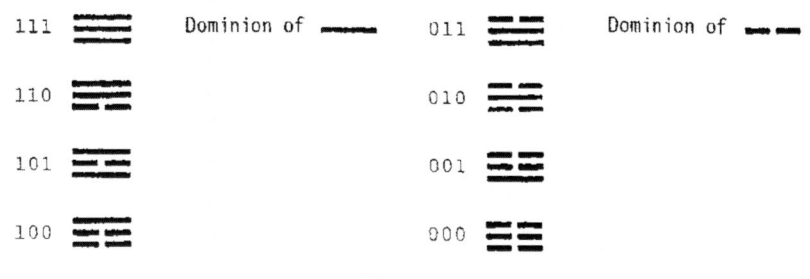

111	⎯⎯	Dominion of ⎯⎯	011	− −	Dominion of − −
110			010		
101			001		
100			000		

Figure 10.9

As Trigrams are already 2 raised to the third power, they can be nicely expressed as a three-dimensional figure (Fig. 10.10). We can see that the top-line of the four upper Trigrams is Yang, therefore the element it 'covers' is under Yang dominion. The four bottom signs have a Yin as top-line, and the element it hovers above is under Yin dominance.

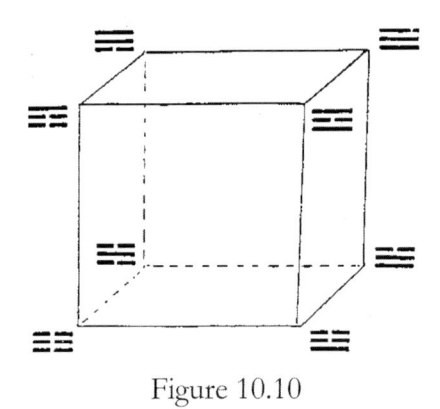

Figure 10.10

A further discussion of building up images from the bottom upwards would lead us into 'Tetragrams', ideally shown in four dimensions. Below (Fig. 1.11) is how we might envision a four-dimensional picture.

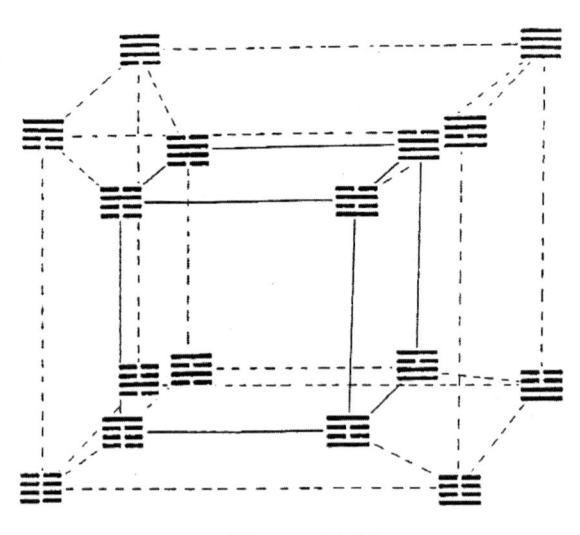

Figure 10.11

Likewise, 'Pentagrams' and Hexagrams, requiring fifth- and sixth-dimensional schemes, cannot be easily expressed geometrically. An attempt to express Hexagrams in a more dimensional form was made by

Z. D. Sung in a terse but exquisite manual on "The Symbols of the Yi King." To fathom the Hexagrams' parallel dimensions, we **turn over** the tortoise shell (Fig. 10.12), whose gift is to remind us of life's mysteries. **As above, so below;** to find life's many patterns and paths we must also look under the surface! The visible, Yang **shell** manifests the invisible, Yin force moving up from below, and out from within.

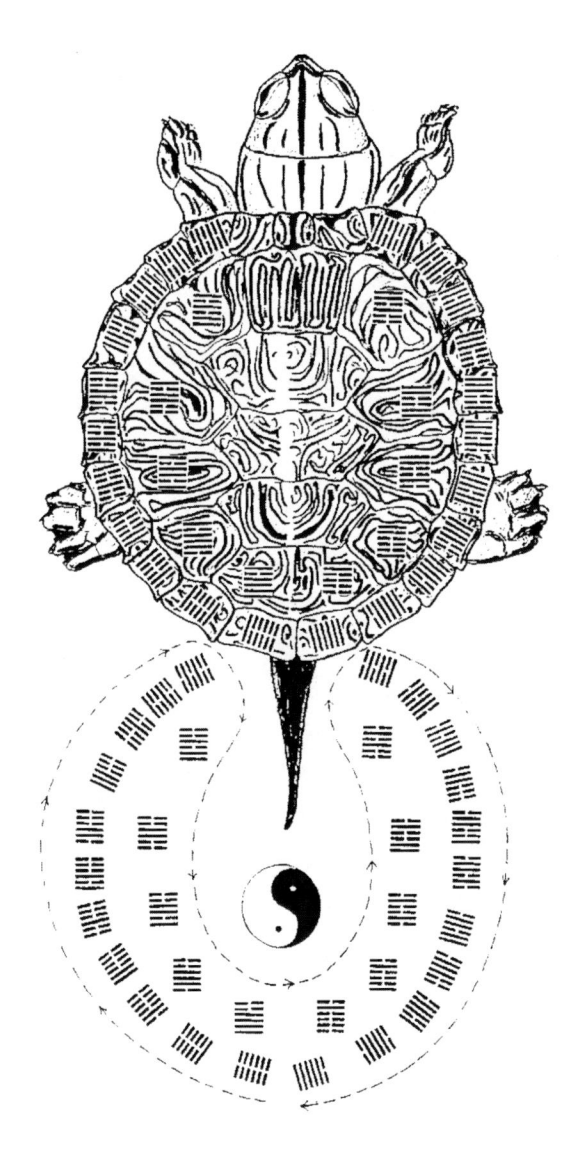

Figure 10.12

May this poetic and artistic tribute to life's infinite, miraculous and mysterious forces (Fig. 10.13), guide you forward as we end our tale!

```
                     Who's
                  whispering,
               coming toward us?
              Maybe it's a tortoise?
            Yes!  Now I am listening...
     Though I speak not in rhymes, Nor am I likely to be wordy,
     My home's a fortress sturdy    That is with me at all times.
     There is no shame in crawling, Nor in retreating to my shell,
     Where I am sure to remain well Without a fear of ever falling.
     I am not built to win a race,  But I know it doesn't matter.
     Nature has no need to flatter. She has blessed me with grace.
     What have I learned of life?   It's a journey one must take,
     Sometimes swimming in a lake,  Sometimes overcoming strife.
       My eggs are laid with care   So the line of my creation
       Can last beyond my station.  That is my hope and prayer.
        If home is in one's heart,  Then you see my heart shown
        in my carapace I've grown   As I've worn from the start.
                  My humble species has evolved
                  Through many ages upon Earth,
                     Believing in the honest
                        worth... Of riddles
                          given to be
                            solved
                              !
```

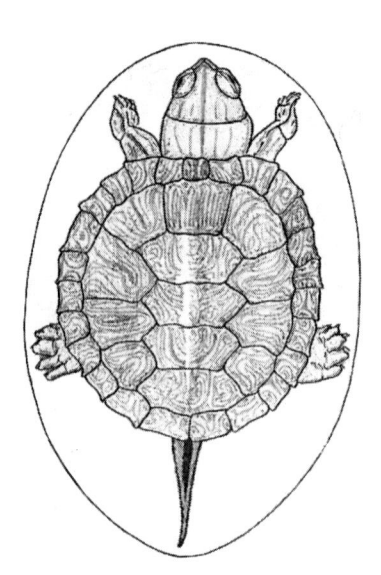

Figure 10.13

APPENDIX: MODELS FOR FURTHER STUDY

The following models, and pages of Hexagram Cards, are provided for I Ching students and researchers to practice the various methods introduced within this text. With perseverance comes success!

The arrows in the first dotted circle show the usual direction of forward movement through a Triole. Place your Hexagrams in the blank spaces. Across the top: Head left, Shell right. The Tail Hexagram belongs in the central space below.

Original Triole in Forward Flow:

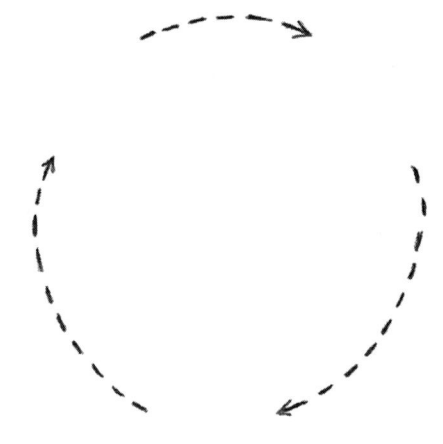

The same Triole in Reverse Flow:

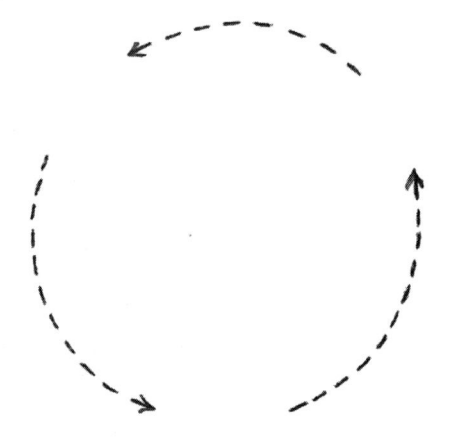

This Logon has Hexagram 2 in the center of the star. Place your Original Triole as before. Solid-line arrows through H 2 point to where to place the Reverse Hexagrams.

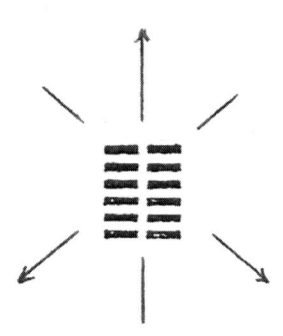

This next Logon has Hexagram 1 in the star's center. Place your original Triole as before, then follow the arrows through H 1 to form three new Hexagrams. Your Original Triole is your 'Drama' Triangle; the three new Hexagrams form the 'Power' triangle.

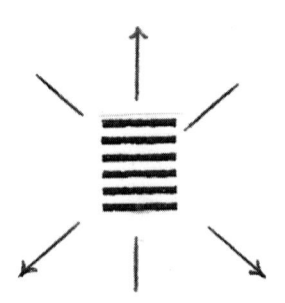

This Logon has 7 blanks. Place your Original Triole in the Drama Triangle 'Codon'; the Sum Hexagram in the center of the star. The arrows point to your Power Triangle Hexagrams, or 'Pokon'.

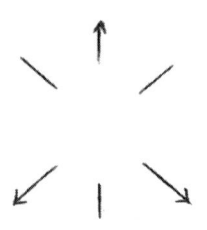

Put your Original Triole in the central blank spaces of the curved triangle, and put the Interim Hexagrams on the loops of Un-time:

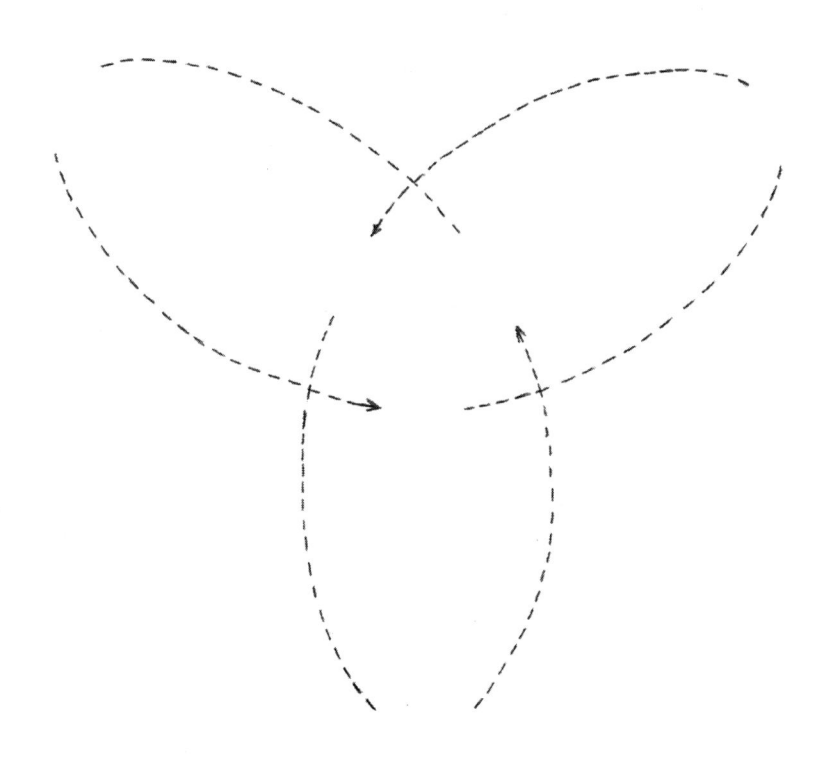

This form can be used as is, or turned on its corner to explore the many relationships between Hexagrams in the Standard Square.

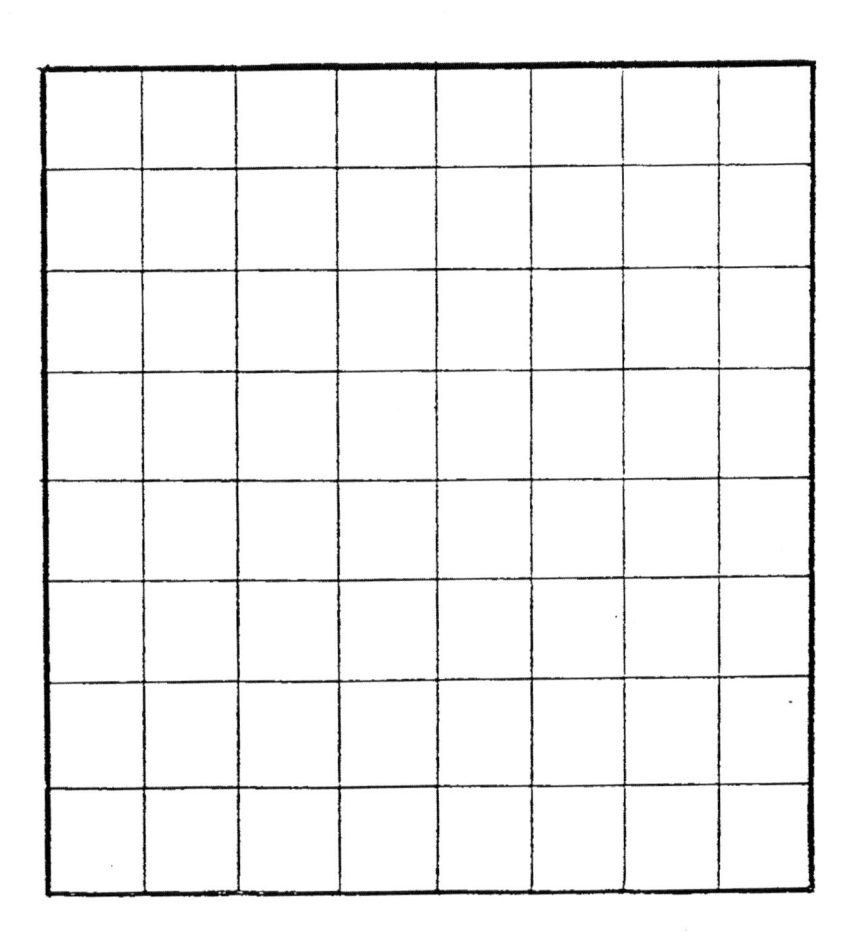

GLOSSARY

Bigram: One of four possible combinations of the monograms, also associated with the four compass points and four elements.

Binary System: Base two numbering sequence, reflected in unmarked Hexagrams, showing only Yin or Yang lines.

Block: Four Hexagrams formed by two pairs of inverted and opposite Hexagrams.

Changing Line: Any Yang or yin line in one Hexagram that becomes its opposite at the same level of a subsequent Hexagram. Changing lines carry 'marks' to indicate the change.

Codon: A set of dots placed in the form of a downward triangle.

Co-Index: The number of changing lines marked in a Hexagram.

Conversion: Two Hexagrams having opposite lines at the same levels.

Division: A group of Trioles with a common Tail Hexagram.

Drama Triangle: Hexagrams in a Codon formation. Regarding an oracle question, it symbolizes the earthly drama surrounding the seeker at the time.

Duplets: Two strokes that follow each other on any given level.

Elements: Symbolic meanings of Fire, Earth, Air and Water.

Emperor: The center stroke of a Triplet. Also, the Sum Hexagram of a Triole, placed in the center of a Star pattern. In a linear row of seven Hexagrams, the Emperor is in the middle, between a Triole and a Tri-une.

Forward Triole: The customary flow of Hexagrams from Head to Shell to Tail, signifying a future-oriented perspective of time.

Greater Heaven: The symbolic meaning of the complete set of 4096 Trioles, whose moving forces suggest a parallel to the planetary movements of our solar system.

Head Hexagram: The first Hexagram of a Triole sequence, normally appearing with marks derived using a method such as throwing coins.

Hexagram: Any combination of yin or Yang lines in a series by 'stepping up' or 'stepping down' through six levels, signifying a compression of six separate Time-quanta into one Time-quantum.

Interim Hexagrams: These occur in Un-Time, derived by translating the quaternary differences between Hexagrams into a new Hexagram image, symbolizing a gift of guidance for one's situation.

Inversion: Two Hexagrams whose lines flow in an opposite sequence of Yin and Yang from top to bottom.

Law of Odd and Even (or the Odd-Even Rule): combining anywhere Yang = Odd, and Yin = Even, results in a third line. Thus, 2 Yangs = Yin; 2 Yins = Yin; and 1 Yang + 1 Yin = Yang.

Level: The vertical placement of a yin or Yang line in a Hexagram, where Level 1 = the bottom line and Level 6 = the top line.

Lines of Text: The symbolic commentary pertaining to the various changing yin or Yang lines of any Hexagram. Its reading offers the questioner guidance.

Logon: A circle of six dots, marking where six Hexagrams may be placed.

Marks: Shown by an 'x' in the middle of a yin line, or '0' in the middle of a Yang line, they indicate the line's changing nature.

Matrix: The square table of 8 lower and 8 upper trigrams, combined with each other to give each of the 64 possible Hexagram numbers.

Monogram: The single expression of the principles of Yin (__ __) or Yang (_____) .

Negative Logic: The Tri-une flow changes, opposite to the Odd/Even Rule: ___ + ___ = ___ ; _ _ + ___ = _ _ ; and _ _ + _ _ = ___ .

Nominee: The first stroke of a Triplet, reflecting a Binary count. If Yin, then the triplet's binary value is 0, 1, 2 or 3. If Yang, then the triplet's binary value is 4, 5, 6 or 7. The Nominee has dominance over the other strokes, as the top line of a trigram, and top line of a Hexagram.

Octonary: A Triplet numbering system, assigning values from 0 - 7 to the same 8 possible combinations of 3 yin and Yang lines as form the trigrams.

Oracle: The correlation of various Hexagrams with meaningful commentary, offering guidance and predicting outcomes associated with a question posed.

Original Triole: The Triole formed in the usual way, whereby a Head Hexagram is first obtained, which becomes the Shell, then the Tail.

Pairs: Two Hexagrams having a special relationship of inversion or conversion.

Pokon: A set of dots placed in the form of an upward pointing triangle.

Power Triangle: Hexagrams in a Pokon formation. Regarding an oracle question, it symbolizes Heavenly influences available to a receptive seeker.

Quaternary System: Uses base 4, expressed in the I Ching through changing lines where 0 = Yin, 1 = Yang, 2 = changing yin and 3 = changing Yang. Based on marks, a Hexagram's quaternary value goes from 0 to 4095.

Reverse Triole: A Triole with lines that are marked to show a reverse flow from an Original Triole, signifying a past-oriented perspective in time.

Rolling: The triplet flow, where the first and third strokes are the same.

Shell Hexagram: The middle Hexagram of a Triole, derived from the Head Hexagram and leading to the Tail.

Smaller Heaven: A symbolic association with the Binary flow of yin and Yang lines, stepping up or down to form one of 64 Hexagrams, analogous to the Lunar phases and earthly changes.

Square: See Matrix.

Star Pattern: A pattern of Trioles in the standard square as well as one derived from forming certain Trioles into a Logon.

Sum-Cell: A grouping of Trioles, whose Sums repeat a pattern.

Sum Hexagram: A new Hexagram image obtained by adding the three Triole numbers and reducing them by 4095, if necessary. Placed in the center of a Logon, it signifies the central issue.

Tail Hexagram: The third Hexagram of a Triole, derived from the Shell, and which becomes the Head.

Time-line: The ongoing perception or psychological experience of events and their meanings.

Time-quantum: The smallest amount of perceivable and measurable time.

Time value: The subjective experience of time which gives life meaning, (i.e.. passive, strong or weak), and expressed in the I Ching by Yang or Yin lines.

Trigram: A combination of three yin or Yang lines, also associated with the eight compass directions and traditional family roles.

Triole: A set of three Hexagrams whereby any two Hexagrams combine to form the third. There are 4096 possible Trioles.

Triole Groups: Taking repetitions into account, 1365 Trioles form 6 Groups. Groups are divided into Cells, which are sub-sets of 4 Trioles. Cells share certain characteristic patterns.

Triplets: The three strokes of any level of a Triole or Tri-une.

Tri-une: The three Tail Hexagrams of the Trioles formed across the central Sum Hexagram of a Logon; or any 3 Hexagrams, chosen together at random.

Un-Time: That which occurs between perceivable quanta of time.

Utmost Heaven: A cubic system of 64 x 64 x 64, symbolizing the complexity of the stars or the 'whole' universe of possibilities, whose key is understanding the many Triole inter-relationships.

Wu: A Chinese word signifying that state of which we know nothing.

Wu-Chi: A symbolic dotted circle around Wu from which the Universe is said to have emerged.

Yang: The active, moving, creative, male principle (not intended to be gender biased), expressed as the monogram: _____

Yang-flow: The sequence of changing lines consisting of One yin and two Yang in any order.

Yin: The passive, receptive, female principle (not meant to be gender biased), expressed as the monogram: __ __

Yin-flow: The repetition of the yin line from Head to Shell to Tail, without marks, retaining a value of zero.

THE GIFT OF THE TORTOISE: NEW INSIGHTS INTO THE I CHING

INDEX

Abbreviations, key to, 38-41
Astrological correlates, 110, 123, 151
Astronomical correlates, 31, 110, 123
Binary Reasoning, 16, 20, 107-109, 147; and the elements 29-30; finding the equivalent Hexagram, 38; and Fu-Hsi 30; and Odd/Even Rule 18-25, 80, 89, 98, , 131, 142
Binomial curve, 8, 9, 76
Changes (See Marks), deeper meaning of, 133-135 /and creation, 135 / in triplet, 135
Codon, 122, 125
Coin, numerical element/use of , 17, 27-30
Co-index, 61, 62, 71, 73, 118, 119, 125 (see also Hexagrams)
Cleary, Thomas, 44
Divisions, 72-82, 107, 135 (see also Hexagram pairs)
Duplets, 135
Elements, 6, 7, 28, 29, 107-110, 123, 143-153
Emperor, 130, 131-146
Fu His (circle of, legend of), 17, 50, 77, 126
Greater Heaven, 31, 32, 113, 139
Hua Ching Ni, 133
Hexagram, binary equivalent, 38; cards (see Appendix); Interim, 97-101, 111 numbering, 39; pairs, 51-71; blocking, 74-75; divisions of 76-83 grouped by co-index, 72; number of Yang lines, 74; opposites, 73; and standard square, 49-52, 55-63; in a star pattern, 53, 54; sum, 111
Intentional force, 149-151
Jou Tsung Hwa, 142
King Wen, 17, 51, 55
Logon, 95, 96, 123*
Marks (see also Odd/Even Rule) and binary values, 30, 31; indicating changes, 108, 109, 112, 117; invisible, Wu change, 134; and moving power, 41; origin of symbols, 30; purpose of, 19, 19, 119-120; and quaternary system, 31, 120-122; retained in the 2nd Hexagram, 41; in reverse Hexagrams, 92-95
McKenna, Terrence, 61, 72, 118
Negative logic, 6, 54, 113, 131 - 136, 141
Nominee, 143
Octahedron, 149
Octonary base, 131, 132; triplet code142, 143
Odd/Even Rule, 18-25, 112, 118 (See also Binary Reasoning) opposed to, 142
Oracle, 1, 26-40, 44, 47, 84, 87, 100, 103,-105, 109-110, 114, 118-120, 122, 130, 141, 146, 153
Pairs (see Hexagrams)
Platonic solids, 139
Pokon, 122, 124, 125, 137
Probability Theory, 9-13
Quaternary System (also Trioles), importance of marks 122; trigram values, 87-91
Shao Yung, 50

Smaller Heaven, 31, 50, 51

Sorrell, Roderick and Amy Max, 42

Sum Hexagrams, 111-113, 121-126; Cells, 113-116; key to, 115, 116; ways, illustrated, 128, 129

T'ai Chi, symbol, 31; Tu, 106, 133, from Wu Chi, 139

Tetragrams, 10-12, 154

Tetrahedrons, 31, 139-141, 150

Time, quantifying, Un-time, filling, compressing, stepping in: Chapter 1; circle of experience, 43; coil or spiral, 16, 44, 45, 48; and Interim Hexagrams, 96-101; jump across, 3, 43, 45, 46, 48, 97, 100, 103, 104; line, reviewing 110-111; loops of, 47, 99; meaning of, in reverse Hexagrams 94-96; psychological 48, 87, 95, 97, 104; real, 21-23, 48; as Yin, 45

Tortoise, and coin tossing, 30; and Sum numbers, 126; Amy's drawing of, 127; with Hexagrams 155; with poem, 156

Trigrams, and eight directions, 7; as daughters/sons, 51; as matrix tool, 39, 40, 49; and Smaller Heaven, 50; mirroring and order of, 77-79; mistaken notions about, 106, 153; number values, 132; formation of, 153; in 3 dimensions, 154

Triole, 31; cells, 34-36; groupings, patterns, 32-37; example of, 41; on circle/loops of time, 48; divisions of (see Hexagrams); head, shell, tail 81-83; in drama triangle, 84, 112, 122, 125; meaning of, 109-110; forward and reverse, 110-111; numbers, 120; in power triangle, 85, 112, 113, 117, 118, 122, 125; formation of, 134; with Emperor and Tri-une 144, 145; and quaternary system, 106; 33, 39, 108, 120; set, 87, 88; in reverse, 87-96, 101-102; in star pattern, 82, 112, 119, 122, 123; sums, 111, 122, 123; as yin manifestation, 125; in 3-D model, 137, 138; as tri-unes, 140

Triplets, changing, rolling, and negative logic, 134-136; flow, 137, 142; decimal values, 142, 143; relation to Triole, 144, 145

Tri-une, 113, 131; flow, 136, 137, 141; numbers of 140; triplets 136-137,146

Utmost Heaven, 31, 44, 113, 132, 139

Wu, 106; -change 132, 134, 136; -chi, 106, 134, 135

Yarrow stalks, 29

Yang, binary value, 147; evolution of symbol 26, 106; flow, 117; power of Emperor, 135

Yin, binary value, 147; evolution of symbol, 26, 106; flow 117

Yin/Yang symbol, 64; as infinity, expressed in the Hexagram circle, 65-69

Z.D. Sung, 155

BIBLIOGRAPHY

Adrian, Franciscus, Die Schule des I Ging: 1. Hintengrundwissen, 2. Die Praxis, Diederichs, Munschen, 1994.

Albertson, Edward, The Complete I Ching for the Millions with Illustrations, Sherbourne Press, 1969.

Anthony, Carol K, Guide to the I Ching, Anthony Publishing Company, Stow, Massachusetts, 1980.

Anthony, Carol K, The Other Way: A Book of Experience in Meditation Based on the I Ching, Anthony Publishing Co., Stow, M.A. 1990.

Arguelles, Jose, Earth Ascending: An Illustrated Treatise on the Law Governing Whole Systems, Bear & Company, Santa Fe, New Mexico, 1988.

Barry, Leo Georges, Le Yi King, Base du code Genetigue, DerviLivres, Paris, 1978.

Boering, Hans, I Tjing Handboek, servire, Utrecht,1994.

Blofeld, John, The Book of Change, A New Translation of the Ancient Chinese I Ching with Detailed Instruction for its Practical Use in Divination, George Allen & Unwin Ltd, London, 1965.

Borkent, J, DNA & I Tjing: Een studie naar de betekenis van hun opmerkelijke code-overeenkomst, Wen Wang Serie No 1 Zandvoort, 1987.

Cleary, Thomas, I Ching Mandalas: A Program of Study for the Book of Changes, Shambhala Publications Inc., Boston, MA. 1989.

Cleary, Thomas, The Taoist I Ching, Shambala, Boston, London. 1986.

Colmer, Michael, Executive I Ching, The Business Oracle, Blandford Press, Poole Dorset, 1987.

Crowley, Aleister, The I Ching: A New Translation of the Book of Changes, Level Press. San Francisco, 1971.

Culling, T.Louis, The Incredible I Ching, Samuel Weiser, NY, 1969.

Culling, Louis, The Pristine Yi King: Pure Wisdom of Ancient China, Llewellin Publications, St. Paul, MN, 1989.

Dhiegh, Khigh Alx, The Eleventh Wing: An Exposition of the Dynamics of I Ching for Now, Nash Publishing Corp., Los Angeles, CA, 1973.

Douglas, Alfred, The Oracle of Change: How to Consult the I Ching, Victor Collancz Ltd, London, 1971.

Eason, Cassandra, I Ching Divination for Today's Women, Foulsham, NY.

Farrington Hook, Diana, The I Ching and You, Routledge, & Kegan Paul, London and Boston, MA 1973.

Farrington Hook, Diana, The I Ching and Its Associations, Routledge & Kegan Paul, London, Boston and Henley, 1975.

Farrington Hook, Diana, The I Ching and Mankind, Routledge & Kegan Paul, 1975.

Fiedeler, Frank, Die Wende: Ansatz einer Genetischen anthropologier nach dem system des I Ching, Werner Kristkeitz Verlag, 1979.

Govinda, Anagarika, The Inner structure of the I Ching, Book of Transformation, Wheelwright Press, San Francisco, CA, (?).

Grafe, E.H., Die acht urbilder, des I Ging, Hugo Grafe verlag 637 Oberstedten /Oberursel Ts., 1968.

Grafe, E.H., I Ging, buch des stetigen und der wandlung, Hugo Grafe Verlag, Oberstedten / Oberursel, 1967.

Granet, Marcel, La pens, Chinoise edition Albin Michel, Paris, 1968.

Hacker, Edward, Ph.D., The I Ching Handbook: A Practical Guide to Logical and Personal Perspectives From the Ancient Chinese Book of Change, Paradigm Publications, Brookline, MA, 1993.

Heuzen, Joop van, De I Tjing gids, Kosmos 28 K Uitgevers, Utrechtj Antwerpen.

Hoefler, Angelika, I Ching: New Systems, Methods and Revelations: An Innovative Guide for All of Life's Events and Changes, Lotus Light Publications, USA, 1988.

Hopen, Peter ten, I Ching, Het boek van de verandering, Kosmos Uitgevers, UtrechtjAntwerpen, 1985.

Houa, Liou Tse, La cosmologie des pa Koua et l'astronomie moderne:
situation embryonaire du soleil et de la lune prevision d'une nouvelle planete, Librairie de Medicis Paris, 1940.

Jou, Tsung Hwa, The Tao of I Ching Way to Divination, Tai Chi Foundation, Taiwan, 1984.

Kegan, Frank R., I Ching Primer; An Introduction to the Relevant Process, Perspective Upon the Occult in General and the Flux Tome (I Ching) in Particular, The Aries Press, Chicago, 1979.

Kiang, Koh Kok, The I Ching: An Illustrated Guide to the Chinese Art of Divination, Illustrated by Tan Xiaochun Asiapac Books, Pte Ltd., Singapore, 1993.

Kuang, Yuan, I Ging: Praxis Chinesischer Weissagung, otto Wilhelm Barth Verlag, Munchen - Planegg, 1951.

Legge, James, I Ching. Book of Changes. Edited with Introduction and Study Guide by Ch'u Chai with Winberg Chai, University Books, Inc. NY, 1969.

Leichtman, Robert R. and Carl Japikse, Healing Lines: A New Interpretation of the I Ching for Healing Inquiries, Ariel Press, Columbus, OH, 1989.

Leightman, Robert R. and Carl Japikse, Ruling Lines: A New Interpretation of the I Ching for Making Intelligent Decisions - Professionally & Personally, Ariel Press, Columbus, OH, 1990.

Liu, Da, I Ching Coin Prediction: How to Consult the I Ching to Predict Your Future, Harper & Row, NY, Evanston, San Francisco, London, 1975.

MacHovec, Frank J., I Ching: The Book of Changes, The Peter Pauper Press, Mount Vernon, NY, 1971.

Maela & Patrick Paul, Le chant sacre des energies, Musique, Acupuncture, tradition, Editions Presence, Sisteron, 1983.

Marchall, Pease, The Aguarian I Ching, Brotherhood of life Inc., Albuquerque, NM, 1993.

Markert, Cristopher, I Ching: The No. 1 Success Formula, Let This Time-tested Method Help You Make The Right Decisions - Today!, The Aquarian Press, Wellingborough, Northamptonshire, 1986.

Marolleau, Jean, La symboligue chinoise, Dervy-Livres, Paris, 1978.

Marolleau, Jean, La Galaxie yin Yang, ou Ie triomphe de la forme, Robert Dumas, Paris, 1975.

McCaffree, Joe E., Bible and I Ching Relationships, South Sky Book Co., Hong Kong, 1982.

McCaffree, Joe E., Divination and the Historical and Allegorical Sources of the I Ching, The Chinese Classic or Book of Changes, Miniverse Services, Los Angeles, CA.

McClatchie, Canon, A Translation of the Confucian I Ching or The Classic of Change, with notes and appendix, Ch'eng Wen Publishing Company, Taipei, 1973.

McKenna, Terence K. and Dennis J., The Invisible Landscape: Mind, Hallucinogens and the I Ching, The Seabury Press, NY, 1975.

Mears, I. and L.E., Creative Energy. A Study of the I Ching, Ohara Publications, Inc. Burbank CA, 1976.

Mesker, Harmen, The I Tjing in ons leven: Een moderne en verhelderende uitleg van het klassieke orakel, Schors Uitgeverij, Amsterdam, 1996.

Melyan, Gary G. and Wen-kuang Chu, I Ching, The Hexagrams Revealed, Charles E Tuttle Company, Rutland, & TOkYo, Japan, 1977.

Mesker, Harmen, De I Ching in Ons Leven, uitgeverij Schors Amsterdam, 1996.

Moller, Monique, I Tjing: Het Boek der Onveranderlijk Werkelijkheid, Miranda Uitgevers B.V. Wassenaar, 1985.

More, Steve, The Trigrams of Han: Inner structures of the I Ching, Aquarian Press, Northamptonshire, England 1989.

Murphy, Joseph, Secrets of the I Ching, Parker Publishing Co. Inc., West Nyack, NY, 1970.

Ni, Hua-Ching, I Ching: The Book of Changes and the unchanging Truth, Seven Star Communications Group Inc. Santa Monica, CA, 1994.

Nimwegen, Gerry van, I Tjing in beeld: Een omzetting van de tekens in beelden, Ankh Hermes Bv. Deventer, 1977.

Offermann, Peter H., Das alte Chinesische Orakel und Weisheitsbuch . I Ging, Konflikten klaren, Zweifel losen, Den besseren Weg wahlen, Eine moderne Interpretation, Walter Verlag, AG Olten, 1975.

Omen Press, Essential Changes: The Essence of The I Ching, Omen Press, Tucson, Arizona, 1973.

Oshiro r Hide, The Graphic I Ching, Turtle Island Press, Philadelphia, PA, 1978.

Pattee, Rowena, Moving with Change: A Woman's Re-integration of the I Ching, Arkana, Routledge & Kgan Paul, London, 1986.

Perrottet, Oliver, The Visual I Ching: A New Approach to the Ancient Chinese Oracle with Cards and Commentary, Salem House Publishers, Topsfield, MA, 1987.

Ponce, Charles, The Nature of the I Ching: Its usage & Interpretation, Award Universal Publishing and Distribution Corp., NY, 1970.

Powell, Neil, The Book of Change: How to Understand and Use the I Ching, Orbis Publishing Limited, London, 1979.

Praag, H. van, Sleutel tot the I Tjing, Uitgeverij Kluwer, N. V. Deventer, 1972.

Reifler, Sam, I Ching: A New Interpretation for Modern Times, Bantam Books Inc., NY, 1974.

Richmond, Nigel, Language of the Lines: The I Ching Oracle, Wildwood House, London, 1977.

Riseman, Tom, Introduction to the I Ching, The Book of Changes: The History and Use of the World's Most Ancient System of Divination, The Aquarian Press, Wellingborough, Northamptonshire, 1980.

Ritsema, Rudolf and Karcher, Stephen, I Ching: The Classic Chinese Oracle of Change; The First   Complete Translation with Concordance, Element Books Ltd., 1994.

Roding, Gerlinde, Erkenne das Urbild Suche das Mass: Die Weisheit der Entsprechung I Ging, Herder Freiburg Verlag Breigau, Germany, 1985.

Schoenholtz, Larry, New Directions in the I Ching: The Yellow River Legacy, University Books Inc. Secaucus, NJ, 1975.

Schonberger, Martin, The I Ching & The Genetic Code: The Hidden Key to Life, ASI Publishers Inc., NY, 1979.

Schonberger, Martin, Verborgener Schlussel zum Leben, Weltformel I-Ging im Genetishcn Code, Otto Wilhelm Bart 1973.

Seabrook, Myles, Twelve channels of the I Ching: Ancient Divination for 21st Century, Blandford, London, 1994.

Secter, Michael, Das I Ging Handbuch: Eine Practische Anleitung Zum Besseren Verstandnis, Diedericks Verlag, Germany, 1991.

Shchutskii, Julian K., Researches on the I Ching, Bollingen Series LXII, Princeton University Press.

Sherrill, W.A. and Chu, W.K., An Anthology of I Ching, Routledge & Kegan Paul London, Henley and Boston, 1978.

Sherrill, W.A. and Chu, W.K., The Astrology of the I Ching, Routledge & Kegan Paul. London and Henley, 1976.

Sherrill, Wallace Andrew, Heritage of Change: A Background to Chinese Culture and Thinking, East West Eclectic Society Taipei, Taiwan, 1972.

Shima, Miki, The Medical I Tjing, Blue Poppy Press, Boulder, CO, USA.1992.

Shimano, Jimmei, oriental Fortune Telling, Charles E. Tuttle Co, Publishers, Tokyo, Japan, 1965.

Siu, R.G.H., The Man of Many Qualities: A Legacy of the I Ching, The MIT Press Cambridge, MA, and London Eng, 1968.

Sneddon, Paul, Self-development with the I Ching: A New Interpretation, Foulsham, NY, 1990.

Sorrell, Roderic and Amy Max, An Idiot's Guide to the I Ching, Bio Ching Publishing, Bisbee, Arizona, 1992.

Sterling, Marysol Gonzalez, I Ching and Transpersonal Psychology, Samuel Weiser Inc. York Beach, Maine, 1995.

Stable, Piere, La Kabbale et lew Yi-King, Dervi-Livres, Paris, 1978.

Sung, S.D., The Text of Yi King, (and its appendixes), Chinese original with English translation, Paragon Book Reprint Corp., NY, 1969.

Sung, S.D., The Symbols of the Yi King or The Symbols of the Chinese Logic of Changes, Tat, Wei. An exposition of the I Ching, Institute of Cultural Studies, Taiwan, 1970.

Tawnm, Kim, Le Yi-Chou ou l'art d'interpreter les 64 Hexagrammes, Guy Tredaniel, Edition de la maisnie, Paris, 1978.

Thatcher, Hale, Images of Change: Paintings on the I Ching, E.P. Dutton & Co, Inc. NY, 1979.

Thieffry, Yves, Les. secrets de l'asrologie du Yi King, Elsevier SequoIa, Paris, Bruxelles, 1976.

Venerius, Willem, Lijn in the I Tjing: Omgaan met het Klassieke Book, Uitgevery Ankh-Hermes, BV Deventer, 1991.

Walker, Barbara G., The I Ching of the Goddess, Harper, San Francisco, CA, 1986.

Walker, Brian Browne, The I Ching: Book of Change; A Guide to Life's Turning points, St. Martin's Press, NY, 1992.

Waltham, Clae, Wang, Pi, The Classic of Changes Translated by Lynn John, Columbia University Press, 1994.

Whincup, Gregory, Rediscovering the I Ching, St. Martin's Press, Griffin, NY, 1986.

Wilhelm, Hellmut, Heaven, Earth, and the Man in the Book of Changes, University of Washington Press, 1977.
Wilhelm, Hellmut, Sinn des I Ching, Diedericks Verlag, Germany, 1988.
Wilhelm, Richard, The Secret of the Golden Flower: A Chinese Book of Life, Routledge & Kegan Paul, London, 1996.
Wilhelm, Richard, The I Ching, or Book of Changes, Routledge & Kegan Paul Ltd., 1971.
Williams, Ann, Images from the I Ching: Visual Meditations on the Book of I Ching, Prism Press, Dorset, England, 1987.
Yan, Johnson F., DNA and the I Ching: The Tao of Life, North Atlantic Books, Berkeley, CA, 1991.
Young Lee, Jung, Patterns of Inner Process, The citadel Press, 1976.
Young Lee, Jung, Understanding The I Ching, University Books Inc., New Hyde Park, NY, 1971.
Young Lee, Jung, The I Ching and Modern Man: Essays on Metaphysical Implications of Change, University Books, Inc. Secaucus, NJ, 1975.

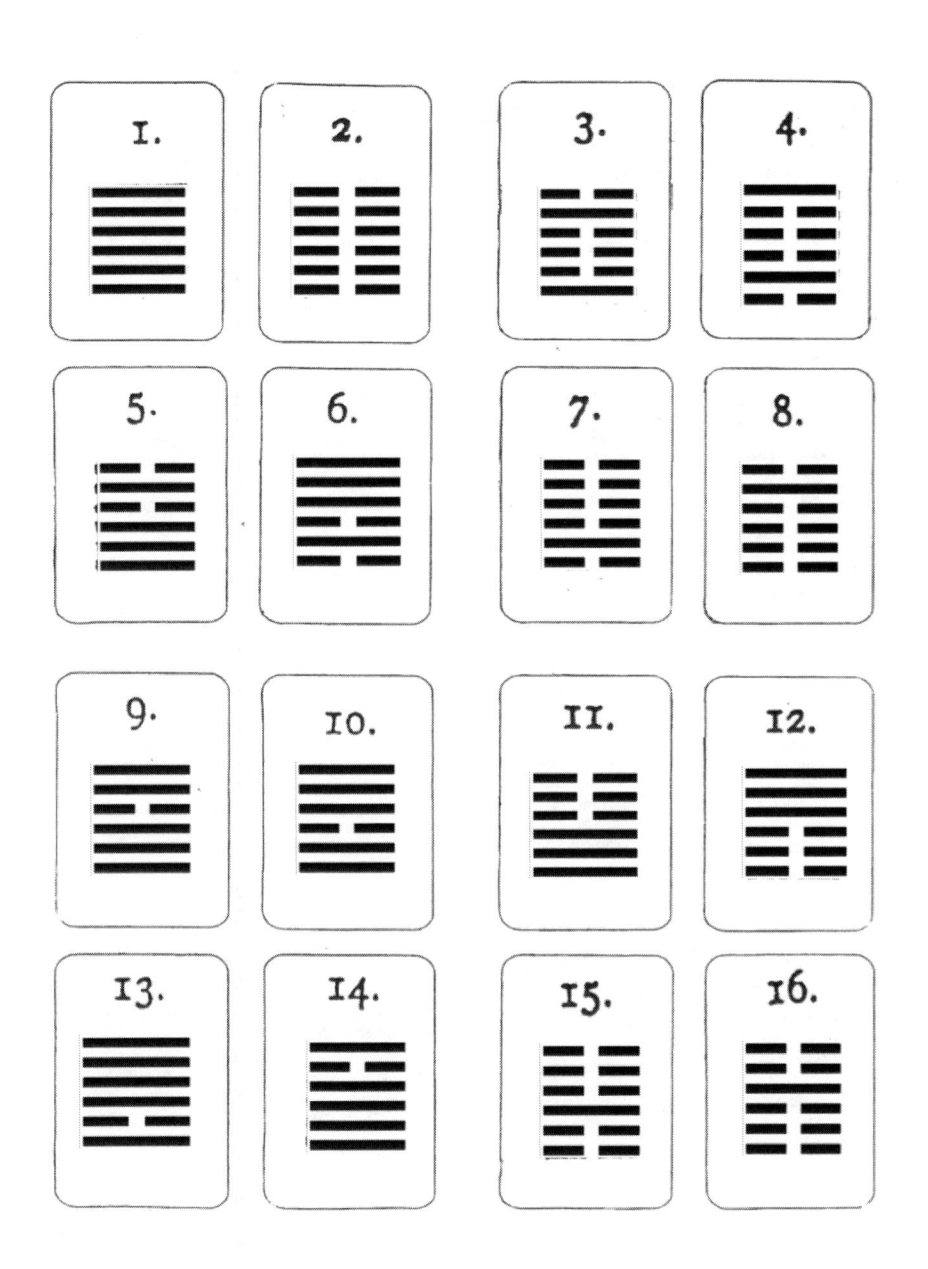

THE GIFT OF THE TORTOISE: NEW INSIGHTS INTO THE I CHING

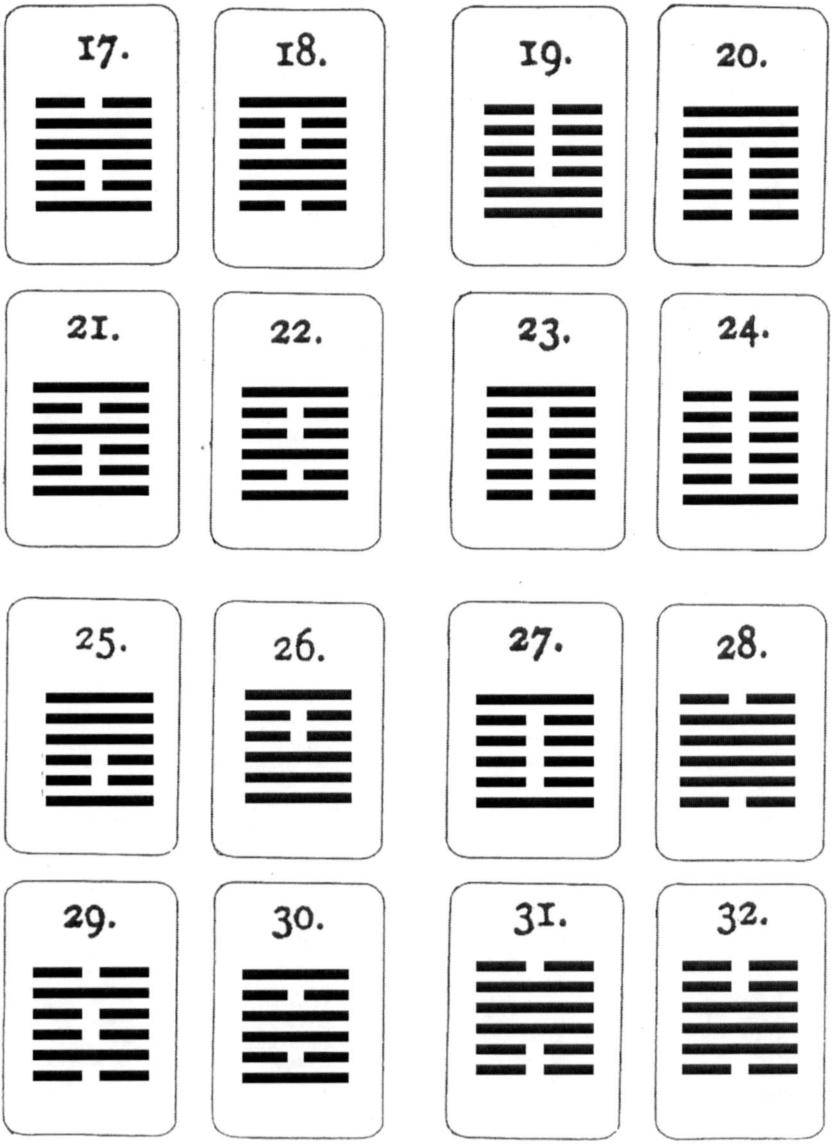
17.
18.
19.
20.
21.
22.
23.
24.
25.
26.
27.
28.
29.
30.
31.
32.

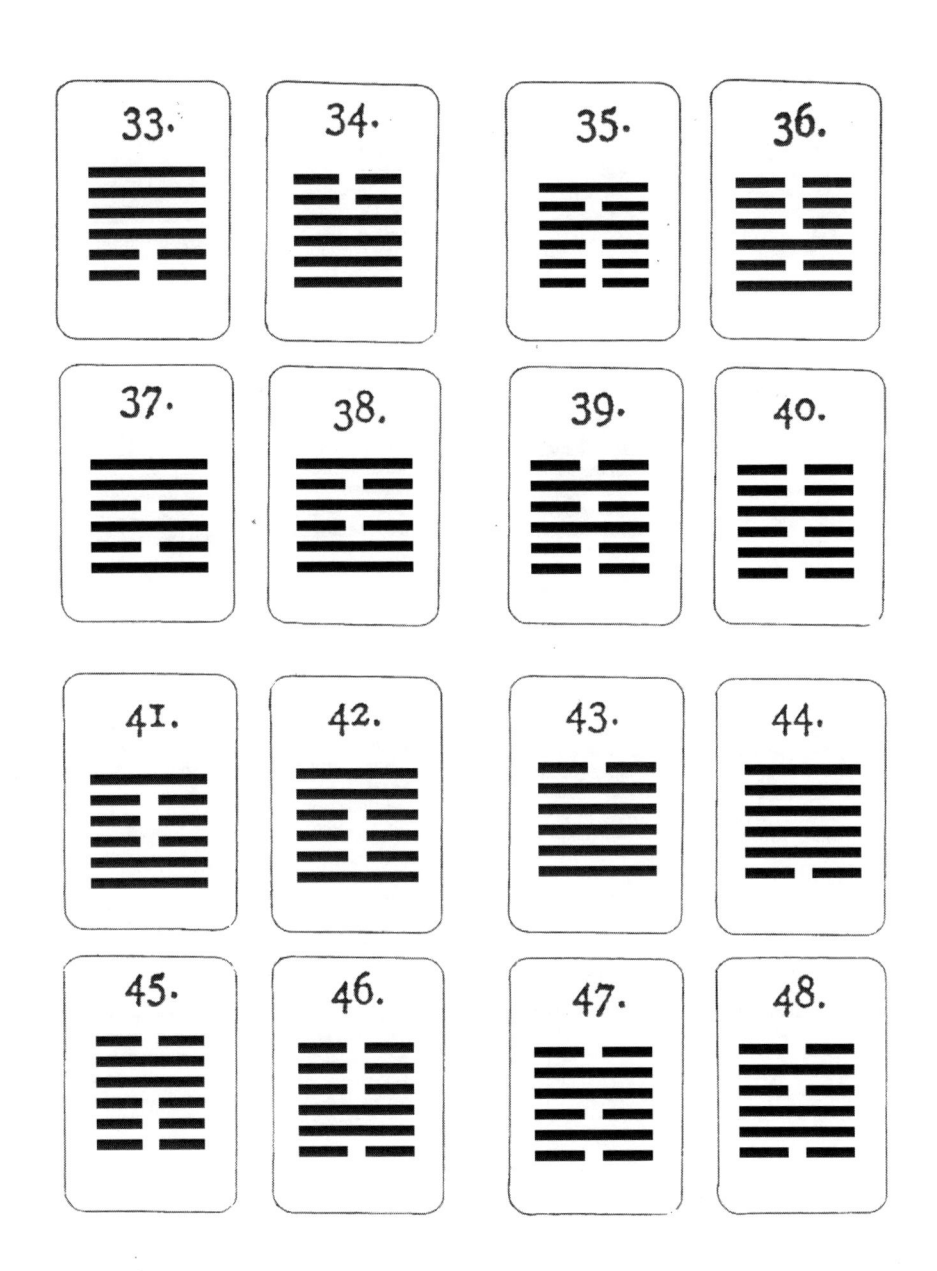

THE GIFT OF THE TORTOISE: NEW INSIGHTS INTO THE I CHING

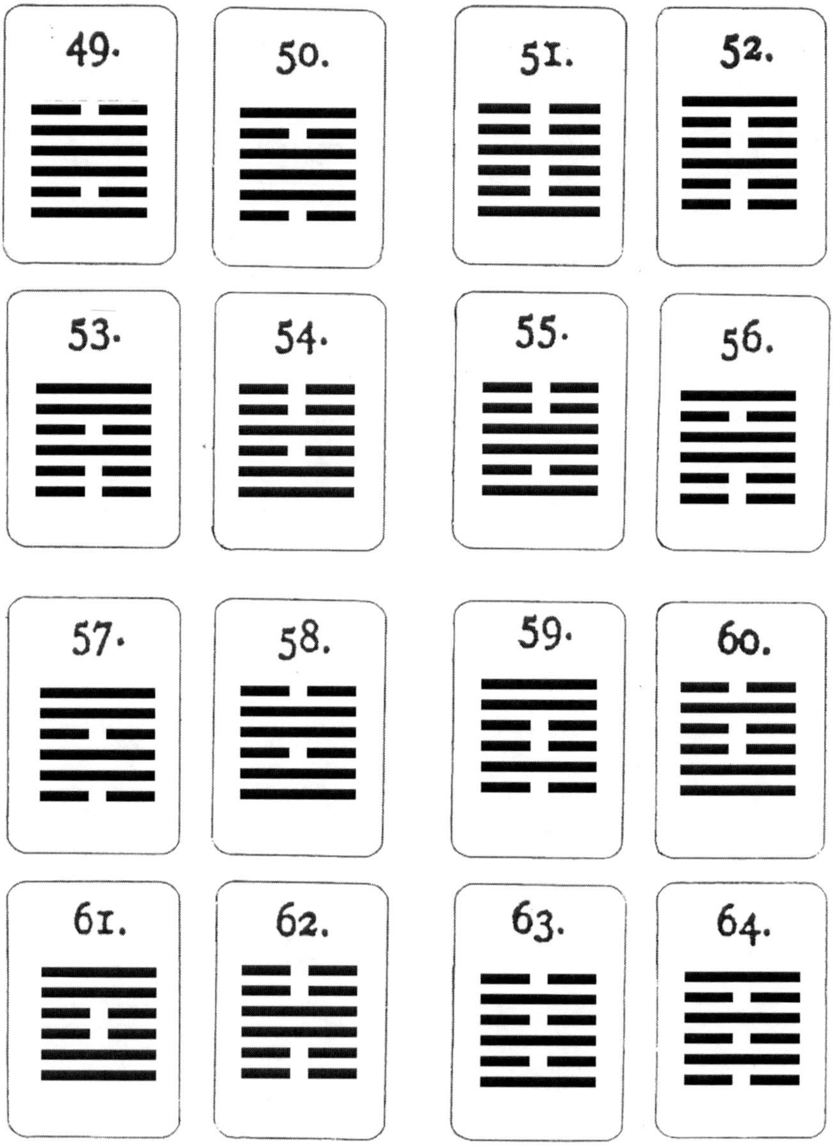
49.
50.
51.
52.
53.
54.
55.
56.
57.
58.
59.
60.
61.
62.
63.
64.

ABOUT THE AUTHORS

All spiritual seekers 'cross great waters.' Jo Onvlee and Amy Shapiro crossed the Atlantic three times between America and the Netherlands in their journey. They first met in 1970, when Amy was in Amsterdam to visit her sister, Claire, who'd been living there for over a year. Jo was skilled in many disciplines; T'ai Chi Chuan, Tarot, Astrology, the I Ching and carpentry, and was learned of a talk at The Kosmos by a lady from America who was an Astrologer, Past Life Therapist, and practitioner of the Awareness Techniques. That summer, they enjoyed many metaphysical and spiritual exchanges in a rare friendship.

A quarter century later, Jo crossed the Atlantic twice to visit America in the 1990's with his son Johan, and daughter Iris, where he gave classes in the coastal city of Gloucester, MA and visited Amy and her husband Ed Kaznocha and sons Jeremy and Clifton. Johan gave wonderful concerts of Dorian musician during those visits as well.

Jo had developed new theories on the I Ching, and Amy had become a writer and editor, and destiny called them to co-author THE GIFT OF THE TORTOISE: NEW INSIGHTS INTO THE I CHING in 1996 and its prequel QUESTIONING THE ORACLE: THE I CHING, in 1997. After a few publishing letdowns, the books sat 15 years until a new millennium brought new challenges, and Seekers in need of Sages.

In 2011, Amy updated both books and at last 'birthed' these twins, culminating a 40-year journey to shine new light on this ancient source of wisdom, inspiration and divination. To learn more about Jo Onvlee and Amy Shapiro, visit NewAgeSages.com.

OTHER *NEW AGE SAGES* BOOKS:

Before This Song Ends: *A Timeless Romance* by Amy Shapiro

The Critique of Pure Music: *Die Kritik Der Reinen Musik*, by Dr. Oskar Adler, Trans: Michaela Meiser; Ed: Amy Shapiro

The DIS-Appointment Book: *A Humor Therapy Guide to Conquering Disappointments,* by Amy Shapiro

Dr. Oskar Adler: *A Complete Man*, by Amy Shapiro

Forces At Work: *Astrology and Career,* by Amy Shapiro

Inviting Eris To The Party: *Our Provocateur In Unfair Affairs,* by Amy Shapiro

It Is ALL Right, by Isabel Hickey

Never Mind, by Isabel Hickey, Jay Hickey and Amy Shapiro

One Sex To The Other: *Reincarnation and the Dual-Gender Soul* By Amy Shapiro

Over The Mountains, by Johan Onvlee and Amy Shapiro

Questioning The Oracle: *The I Ching,* by Jo Onvlee and Amy Shapiro

The Sparrow's Tale: *T'ai Chi Stories to Inspire,* by Johan Onvlee and Amy Shapiro

The Testament of Astrology, by Dr. Oskar Adler (7 Volumes)

Visit NewAgeSages.com to learn about Amy Shapiro's services, her Astrological reports and to contact her for more information.

Made in United States
Cleveland, OH
16 March 2025